WHAT YOUR MOTHER NEVER TAUGHT YOU
THE PIZZA GOURMET WILL!

A collection of gourmet pizzas and upscale accompaniments including all of the dishes from the new PIZZA GOURMET television series on PBS and many more of Chef Carl's favorites that have never before been in print – over 100 recipes in all.

Published by The Pizza Gourmet, Inc.
6005 Executive Drive
Westland, Michigan 48185-1932

Printed in The United States of America
Quebecor Printing Company
Library of Congress Catalog Card Number: 94-93942
ISBN 0-9644550-0-5

Designed by Phillip Collier Designs, Inc.
Typography by Cox Electronic Publishing, Inc.
Photography of food by Steven Mark Needham
Photography of equipment and ingredients by Alan Davidson

First Edition

To my wonderful Jewish parents,
Rose and Ed,
who have been the primary source of
inspiration in my culinary career.

In memory of my dear friend Bette.

ACKNOWLEDGEMENTS

Where would I be without my hard-working and supportive staff! With unfailing enthusiasm they consumed a ton of pizza, endured innumerable trips to the supermarket, and put their private lives on hold in the creation of this cookbook.

Words alone cannot express my gratitude to my two right hands: Cathy Pfeiffer and Deborah Miehlke-Sadlowski. Without the research skills and patience of these talented associates, this book could never have been written.

Special thanks also goes to my friends and colleagues Michael V. Sadlowski and Lawrence Galbraith for all of their help and encouragement.

The edible works of art in the book were photographed in New York by Steven Mark Needham. The easy manner of this brilliant photographer made even long sessions a pleasure.

Finally, I wish to acknowledge my co-author Terri Landry, that able writer and television producer who guided The Pizza Gourmet out of the kitchen and back onto the screen and page.

Chef Carl

FORWARD

Carl Oshinsky, The Pizza Gourmet, has brought back authentic flavors in his repertoire of delicious dishes that the entire family can enjoy. Over the past ten years, his recipes have been favorites in the cooking classes that we offer in our Kitchen Glamor shops. Students return time and time again for his easy and innovative approach to developing new dishes.

Carl has always been extremely generous with our students and has taken the time to assist visiting national celebrities like Giuliano Bugialli, Jacques Pepin and Craig Claiborne.

The Pizza Gourmet brings to life the true meaning of teaching and sharing fine food ideas.

Toula Patsalis

Director of Kitchen Glamor

cooking classes and author of

Pressure Cooker Cook Book

TABLE OF CONTENTS

Given my penchant for pizza, I probably should have been born Pasquale - rather than Carl Oshinsky. If I were the son of an Italian mama named Rosa, instead of a Jewish mother named Rose, I might have learned about the tools of my trade right there at my mother's knee. Instead, everything I know about my favorite food and life's calling I taught myself.

I've spent the past fifteen years catering pizza parties in over 1,000 different homes. Although I also market a line of pizza baking accessories, it is the home catering end of my business that keeps me fresh and in direct contact with my clientele. Clean plates are a great way to get instant feedback! After sampling my gourmet pies, customers typically wander into the kitchen to check out my pizza oven. When all they find is me and a pizza stone, they can't believe their eyes or taste buds. Growing up in suburban Detroit, I was fascinated by our local pizzerias. Ours was a kosher household, and although food for me and my three brothers was plentiful, it was also on the boring side. The only kind of pizza my mother made came from a packaged mix. The end result was a disaster.

Even the pizza we had delivered during family card parties couldn't compare with the paradoxically crisp, yet chewy pizza that was served at the good pizzerias in town. When we ate at those establishments I studied the pizza makers' every move, intent on discovering the key to their heavenly creations.

These pizzeria "scouts" eventually led to the invention of my custom pizza stone. Having made up my mind to become a pizza caterer, I began looking for an element that would allow me to make pizzeria-style pizza in any kitchen.

After experimenting with quarry tiles and various baking stones, I developed THE PIZZA GOURMET Ovenstone. My premium clay ovenstone simulates a professional baking environment in an ordinary home oven.

As unbelievable as it sounds, a home oven with a properly preheated ovenstone can approximate the intense heat of a pizzeria oven. Commercial brick ovens actually have a bit of a disadvantage: they are so wide that every time the door is opened the oven fills with cooler air and the temperature drops. Because home ovens are smaller, cool air doesn't rush in when the door is opened. Similarly, since every time a pizza is placed on a stone it draws the heat away from the baking surface, the constant use of a restaurant oven to bake multiple pizzas lowers the temperature of the slab. In a home oven, where you only bake one pizza at a time, the ovenstone stays hot.

I'm not a restaurateur. I'm not a pizzeria man. As a caterer my avenue for creation has been in home kitchens, so I understand all of the problems that people encounter in that setting. I have experienced, for instance, the vagaries of an oven that doesn't want to get hot. Using methods that I will describe later in this chapter, it is possible to make perfectly respectable pizza, despite an uncooperative appliance. Trust me, you don't have to have a gourmet kitchen to prepare gourmet pizza.

There's a lot of conflicting information and misinformation out there about pizza baking. In quest of the ultimate pizza, people have been wasting their money on special equipment - pans with vent holes, pans with creases, pans with perforations - that simply won't produce the desired result. Many misguided home cooks are also wasting their time searching for THE PERFECT PIZZA DOUGH. Let me state emphatically that a

"Using an ovenstone gives the pizza a sixteenth of an inch skin on the bottom, similar to that of a bagel. You can turn the oven up as high as it goes and the bottom won't burn."

secret recipe for dough simply does not exist. Well-textured, crispy crust depends in large part on the high heat of the oven.

Although the Italians elevated pizza making to an art, pizza in its simplest form - as a flavored disc of bread - has probably been a hot food item since the Stone Age. In their turn, the Egyptians, Etruscans and ancient Greeks all contributed to the cultural lineage of pizza. It wasn't until the nineteenth century, however, that tomato-based pizzas were first baked in the fiery wood-burning ovens of Naples, Italy. Thus, the modern day pizza was launched on its ubiquitous way.

Since the first wave of Italian immigrants arrived in this country before the turn of this century, pizza has steadily increased in popularity until today it ranks right up there with hamburgers and hot dogs as America's favorite food. The annual sales of pizza in restaurants has passed the $20 billion mark, which means that in this country we are consuming over 11 billion slices of pizza each year.

The down side of all this mass consumption of pizza is loss of quality. The neighborhood pizzeria has been replaced by the giant pizza delivery chains, and even though the "Big Three" in the industry are constantly coming up with new products to differentiate themselves, there is an appalling sameness about their menus.

Fortunately, there is a counter revolution going on in the pizza realm. California pizza purveyors have taken the dish in a fresh new direction from the nation's two prevailing regional styles: New York Neapolitan and Chicago deep-dish. Further pushing the envelope are pizza makers in New England and the Southwest who are using indigenous ingredients as toppings. Although the number one pizza in the United States is still pedestrian pepperoni, across the

"The beauty of pizza is its versatility. It's a sort of everyman's food that can be tailored to be as exotic, untraditional or low-calorie as the cook wants — quite unlike greasy take-out pizzas that arrive in cardboard coffins."

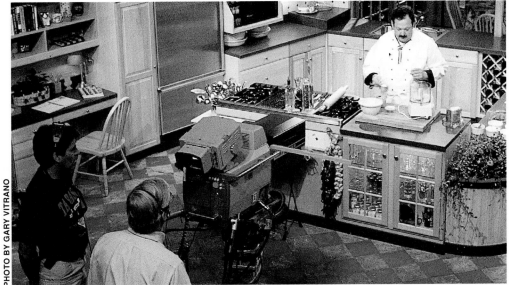

The kitchen of the new PIZZA GOURMET television series, WYES-TV12, New Orleans.

country we are becoming more broad-minded about the dish. Once you accept the notion of pizza without a tomato sauce base, the sky's the limit.

In this book you will find over 100 crowd-pleasing recipes that I use when I cater both large and small functions. A typical menu at one of my pizza parties includes a light pizza or calzone appetizer, a homemade pasta, a salad, a main course pizza and dessert. At home you can mix and match the courses - pairing a light pizza or calzone with a salad, a pasta with a bread, a soup with a salad - to make a meal that matches your family's appetite.

Like the great pizzaiolos - pizza cooks - before me, I take tremendous pride in my product. When people ask me how to make my "edible works of art" I am always happy to share my secrets. There's no mystique to making pizza. Anyone can do it. All it takes is a pinch of knowledge and a dash of desire. You can't go wrong if you remember my motto: Bake it Hot and Bake it Fast!

A.

B.

P.

K.

L.

O.

J.

N.

M.

I.

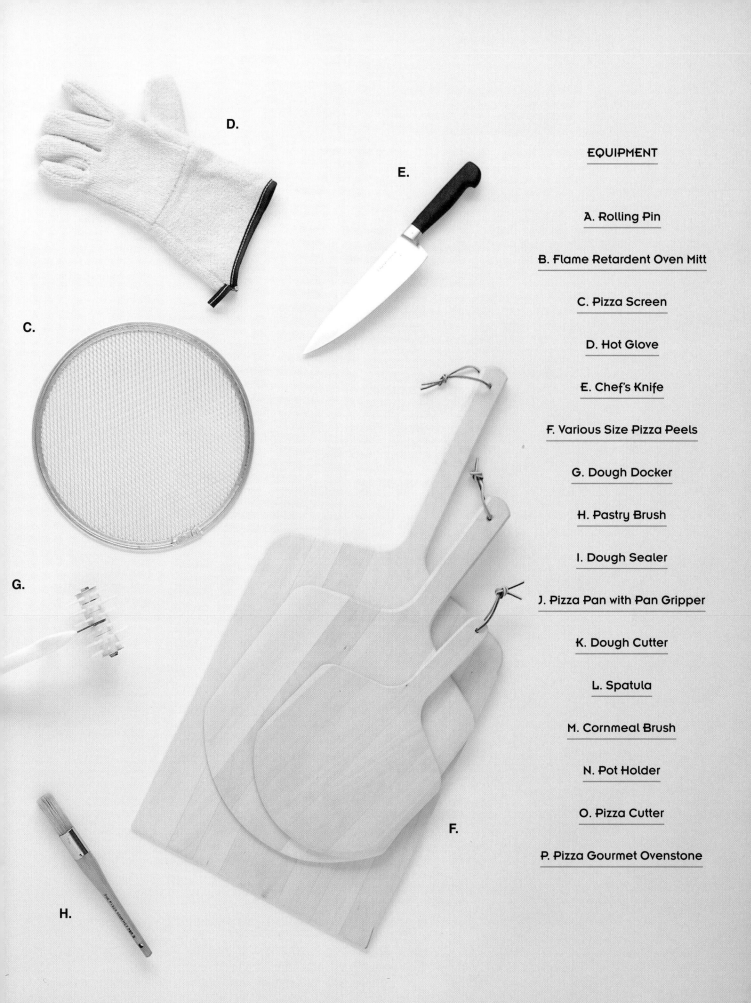

EQUIPMENT

A. Rolling Pin

B. Flame Retardent Oven Mitt

C. Pizza Screen

D. Hot Glove

E. Chef's Knife

F. Various Size Pizza Peels

G. Dough Docker

H. Pastry Brush

I. Dough Sealer

J. Pizza Pan with Pan Gripper

K. Dough Cutter

L. Spatula

M. Cornmeal Brush

N. Pot Holder

O. Pizza Cutter

P. Pizza Gourmet Ovenstone

D.

E.

C.

G.

H.

F.

BAKING STONES

The single most important piece of equipment you need at home for thin, crisp pizzeria-style crust is a baking stone. My PIZZA GOURMET brand ovenstone is made from kiln-fired clay that absorbs twenty per cent of the moisture from the dough. Pizza stones are either round or rectangular and are available in several sizes. Before baking, position the ovenstone on the bottom rack of the oven, then preheat it at 500 degrees F. for one hour. Don't lower the oven temperature; bake the pizza directly on the clay stone at 500 degrees.

PIZZA PEELS

When you use a pizza stone, you also need a pizza peel for transferring your pizzas to and from the oven. These long-handled professional baker's paddles are typically made of either hardwood or metal.

Despite some sources which may tell you otherwise, you do build the pizza directly on the surface of the peel, after first giving it a generous sprinkling of cornmeal. The cornmeal "ball bearings" will allow you to slide the pizza off the peel and onto the stone.

Just before popping the pizza into the oven, jiggle the paddle a little. If the pizza moves, press on. If it doesn't, use my blessing technique, which is to lift the edge of the pizza and toss cornmeal under the areas that are stuck.

At the oven, hold the paddle at a slight angle with the tip of the peel resting on the back of the stone, about 2 inches from the edge. Give the paddle a small jerk and move the pizza onto the stone. When the dough hits the stone it will "grab on" and you can pull the peel right out from under the dough, like the old tablecloth trick. This move takes a bit of practice, so it might be a good idea to bake small pizzas until you get the hang of it. If the pizza doesn't quite clear the edge of the stone, give it a little push back onto the stone with the tip of your peel.

After removing the pizza from the oven, sweep the excess cornmeal from the stone onto the peel using a stiff-bristled cornmeal brush. Discarding any used cornmeal will prevent it from burning and smoking during future baking.

PIZZA SCREENS

If you prefer not to mess around with peels and cornmeal, pizzas can also be shaped and baked on aluminum pizza screens. Wire mesh screens are either round or square and come in several different sizes. The first couple of times you use a new screen, you need to coat it lightly with cooking spray. With use oiling the screen will be unnecessary. Assemble the pizza on the screen and bake it immediately, before it has a chance to rise. For the best results, place the screen directly on a preheated ovenstone and bake. Pizza screens work best with thin rather than thick pizzas.

PIZZA PANS

I only use pans when I make deep-dish style pizza. I prefer heavy deep-dish pans made of tin steel rather than aluminum. This type retains more heat and produces a crispier crust. Aluminum does have its advantages though, in that it's virtually worry-free. Aluminum pans don't need to be seasoned and they never rust.

OTHER PIZZA BAKING TOOLS

Although they are nonessential, food processors and heavy upright mixers with dough hooks make mixing and kneading dough a breeze. If you cook at all, you probably already possess all of the other equipment required for pizza-making. Besides bowls, measuring cups, knives and a cheese grater, I also recommend that you have the following items on hand:

Dough Scraper	Rolling Pin	Pastry Brush
Heat Resistant Gloves and Mitts	Cooling Rack	Pizza Spatula
Pizza Cutting Wheel	Dough Cutter	Scale

My full line of ovenstones and baking accessories is available in kitchenware stores nationwide. For making calzone, or turnovers, you will also need a 4-inch biscuit cutter and a wallpaper seam roller, which is the best gadget I've found for sealing the edges of the dough.

Pasta-making goes hand in hand with pizza baking, but it does require some specialized equipment, most notably a pasta machine for rolling and cutting the dough. Although there are electric models, I prefer the hand-cranked type. Racks and trays for drying fresh pasta are handy, but optional. If you make ravioli, you'll also need a pastry wheel for cutting and sealing the pasta. Another tool for this chore is a ravioli form, which looks a lot like an ice cube tray.

Whether I'm making fettucine, lasagna, farfalle or other fresh pasta, I use the same basic recipe.

BASIC PASTA DOUGH

5 large eggs

3 to 4 teaspoons olive oil

1 teaspoon salt

3 cups unbleached all-purpose flour

Place the eggs, olive oil and salt in the bowl of a food processor; pulse the machine until the mixture is well combined. Gradually incorporate the flour into the dough until it pulls away from the side of the bowl and forms a ball. The pasta dough should not be sticky; depending on the size of the eggs you use, you may need to add more or less flour.

If you don't have a food processor, place the flour in a bowl or on a work surface. Make a well in the center of the flour and break the eggs into it. Add the olive oil and salt, then beat the mixture with a fork, gradually working flour into the liquid until the eggs have been absorbed. Gather the dough into a loose ball and turn it onto a floured board. Knead about 10 minutes until the dough is smooth and elastic.

Divide the dough into thirds and shape each piece into a ball. Flatten a ball of dough and feed it through a pasta machine set on the widest setting. When the dough comes out of the machine, lay it on the counter, fold the edges into the center, and push the air out with your fingertips, working from the bottom to the top of the dough. Repeat this kneading process once or twice, then begin to roll the dough.

Run the dough through the machine a couple of times on each setting - adjusting the rollers so that they are narrower - to the desired thickness of pasta. If the ribbon of dough starts to get sticky, drag it through some flour on the counter. Following the same procedure roll the remaining pieces of dough. When you are through, do not wash your pasta machine!

Let the fresh pasta dry briefly before cutting it into the desired shape. Before you boil it, give your pasta a pinch. If it feels mushy or gummy it needs to dry a little while longer. Generally speaking, by the time your water comes to a boil fresh pasta is ready to use.

Always use twice as much water as pasta and add kosher salt, not oil, to the water. Not only will oil not keep the pasta from sticking, it will coat your pasta so that sauce won't adhere to it. When the pasta first goes into the pot, keep the water moving with a long spoon and then just stand by. Fresh pasta cooks in the blink of an eye.

TOMATOES

When a recipe calls for tomatoes, I generally use either vine-ripened or canned Italian plum tomatoes, or some combination of the two. I'm also partial to the intense flavor of sun-dried tomatoes, so I use them frequently.

As the demand for sun-dried tomatoes has increased, this gourmet item has become available in many supermarkets. Sun-dried tomatoes may be purchased either in dry form or packed in olive oil. Unless they are being added to a liquid medium, such as a sauce, it is necessary to reconstitute the dried variety in hot water before use. For a crunchy garnish, however, crisp sun-dried tomatoes can be minced and sprinkled onto a pizza when it comes out of the oven.

You'll note that nowhere in this pizza book is there a recipe for a basic pizza sauce. I concluded several years ago that as far as pizza goes, cooked tomato sauce is not only unnecessary, it's virtually redundant! As I explain in my cooking demonstrations, any canned tomato sauce you purchase has already been cooked. If you cook it again on top of the stove, that's its second time over the fire. On top of the pizza, it gets cooked yet a third time in the oven. When all is said and done, after all this cooking you end up with less instead of more flavor.

I recommend that you purchase a thick, good-quality tomato sauce and spoon it directly onto the pizza in lieu of making a tomato-based pizza sauce.

OLIVE OIL

Although I use a variety of oils in my recipes, olive oil plays a special role in pizza making. First, I always incorporate a little olive oil into my pizza dough for texture and flavor. Then, when the dough has been shaped on the peel, I often brush olive oil onto the surface to seal it before adding the toppings. Finally, when the pizza comes out of the oven, I like to brush olive oil on the edge for extra flavor and to keep the crust from drying out.

HERBS AND SPICES

Among the seasonings that I regularly add to pizza are oregano, marjoram, Italian parsley and garlic. Like my Italian colleagues, I savor the combination of tomatoes and basil so I grow the herb in my garden. When the basil is ready, I prepare batches of pesto which I freeze and use year-round.

21

FRESH BASIL PESTO

Makes 1 quart.

3 tablespoons pine nuts

1 pound basil leaves, rinsed and well dried

5 garlic cloves

1 tablespoon kosher salt

1 cup freshly grated Parmesan cheese

1 cup olive oil

Toast the pine nuts for several minutes in a dry skillet over medium high heat. When lightly browned, remove the pine nuts from the heat and let cool.

Purée the pine nuts, basil, garlic, salt and Parmesan in a food processor or blender; if all of the basil leaves will not fit into the container, add and process them gradually. With the machine running, slowly incorporate the olive oil until the mixture is smooth. Use the pesto immediately or refrigerate it for up to several days; cover the pesto with a thin layer of olive oil to seal out the air and keep the color vibrant. Pesto may also be frozen indefinitely.

TOP OF THE LINE TOPPINGS

Pizza making requires planning and a well-stocked pantry. Use the freshest ingredients possible; generally speaking that means a last-minute trip to the market for toppings. Choose topping ingredients that compliment each other. You can't just throw a bunch of junk on a pizza and expect it to work; some combinations just aren't appetizing. Sauerkraut, Polish sausage and mozzarella, for instance, are a match made in pizza hell.

Black olives, capers and assorted peppers are just a few of my favorite pizza ingredients. Both sweet and hot peppers must first be roasted, however, to remove their tough skin.

ROASTED BELL PEPPERS OR CHILIES

Roast the peppers over an open flame or in an oven broiler, turning them frequently. When the skin is charred all over, plunge the peppers into ice water. Scrape and pull away the blackened peel, then cut the pepper in half and remove the seeds. Pare the flesh as desired.

SEAFOOD, POULTRY AND MEAT

Pepperoni may be the nation's favorite pizza topping, but due in part to California-style "designer pizzas" and partially in response to the new health consciousness there has been a shift away from traditional meats like sausage, prosciutto, pancetta and Canadian bacon. At the gatherings I cater I now like to offer at least one all-veggie pizza or one topped with fish, shellfish, chicken or turkey.

For traditional deep-dish pizza, however, Italian sausage is practically de rigueur. Although fresh Italian sausage is readily available in most supermarkets, here's my recipe for a delicious homemade version:

ITALIAN SAUSAGE

1 pound cubed pork

1 pound cubed beef

1 tablespoon minced garlic

2 teaspoons fennel seeds

1/2 teaspoon red pepper

2 teaspoons black pepper

2 teaspoons ground coriander

1 to 2 teaspoons salt

"To help eliminate grease, I always precook and drain meat toppings such as sausage, pancetta and bacon before adding them to a pizza. Chilling pepperoni slices before use also makes the pizza less greasy."

Grind the cubed pork and beef together. Place the ground meat in a bowl, then add the remaining ingredients. Mix well. Sauté a spoonful of the sausage mixture in a skillet. When the sample is fully cooked, taste it; if necessary, adjust the seasoning with salt and pepper. Stuff the meat mixture into pork or synthetic casings, tying off the ends. Sauté and slice the sausage, then arrange it on your favorite pizza.

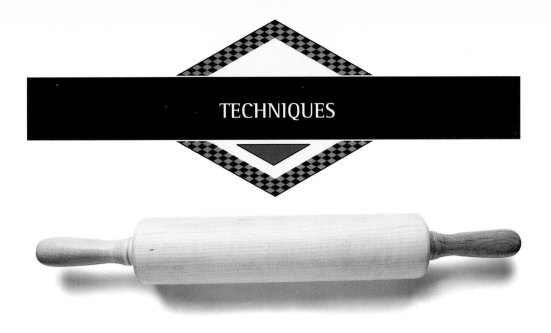

TECHNIQUES

Pizza dough is nothing more than flour, water, yeast, salt and olive oil. Why then, does great pizza crust pose such a challenge?

There are a lot of variables to this deceptively simple equation. By no means is the process of dough making an exact science. The amount of flour you'll wind up using in the dough, for instance, will depend on the amount of moisture in the air. If it's humid in your area, you will need to add more flour, otherwise the dough will be sticky. On the other hand, if the dough seems too dry, you should add a little extra water, but not so much that the dough becomes wet.

Kneading time will depend on whether you make your pizza dough by hand, in a food processor or using an upright mixer. Whichever method you choose, the dough must be worked until it is smooth and pliant.

After mixing and kneading the dough, it should be shaped into a ball and placed in a bowl that has been coated with flour. I flour my bowls instead of oiling them to keep the dough dry. Seal the bowl with plastic wrap and set it in a warm place; ideally this should be a draft-free environment that is 75 to 85 degrees F. in temperature.

BASIC PIZZA DOUGH

Makes 19 ounces of pizza dough.

2 to 2 1/4 cups bread flour

1 teaspoon salt

1 tablespoon olive oil

1 cup plus 2 tablespoons warm water (115 degrees F.)

1 envelope (1/4 ounce) active dry yeast

Place 2 cups of the flour in the bowl of a food processor.

In a small bowl, blend the yeast with the warm water and 1 tablespoon of the flour. Let the mixture stand about 5 minutes to proof the yeast. When it bubbles and foams, pour the yeast mixture through the feed tube into the food processor, with the machine running. Add the olive oil and salt, then incorporate more flour if necessary, until the dough pulls away from the side of the bowl and forms a ball.

Remove the dough from the processor and place it on a floured work surface. Knead the dough for several minutes, working in flour as necessary, until the dough is smooth and elastic and no longer sticky. Shape the dough into a ball and place it into a deep floured bowl. Cover the bowl with plastic wrap, then set it in a warm, draft-free spot to rise.

After two hours the dough can be rolled. For chewier pizzeria-style crusts, however, the dough should be punched down and allowed to rest an additional four hours. The aged or retarded dough can be used immediately or placed in the refrigerator for use the following day. Let chilled dough return to room temperature before rolling it.

Turn the rested dough onto a floured board and press it into a flat circle with your fingers. Do not knead the dough again before rolling it. Shape, top and bake the dough according to the instructions provided in the individual recipes.

For calzone, roll out the pizza dough to about 1/4-inch thick on a floured surface. Cut out circles of dough with a 4-inch round biscuit cutter, then spoon generous tablespoons of filling onto the center of the circles.

Fold the dough over the filling and press the edges together, being careful to keep the edges dry and free of filling. Roll the sealed edges with a wallpaper seam roller to lock in the filling, then pinch and fold the edge in a braiding motion to finish the calzone.

So that they don't get soggy, bake the calzone right away. Place the calzone on a cookie sheet lined with parchment paper or on a lightly oiled pizza screen. Make a small slit on the top of each one to let the steam out as they bake. Bake on an ovenstone preheated to 500 degrees for 10 to 15 minutes. Transfer the baked calzone to a cooling rack and sprinkle them with Romano cheese.

In this book you will find several recipes for focaccia, which is pizza in its most pure, unadorned state. The classic focaccia toppings are simply coarse salt, fresh herbs and olive oil. I have also included a number of more elaborate versions of this flavored bread to serve as snacks or side dishes.

The techniques in this section have never failed me. With practice and perseverance you too can master the art of pizza making.

"Except for the time involved and the convenience, there's really no difference between dough made by hand, dough made in a upright mixer or dough made in a food processor. The key to pizza dough is to start with the quantities of ingredients specified in a recipe, but if the dough is sticky add more flour. Know when to start and stop."

LIGHT PIZZAS AND CALZONE

LOW–FAT TOMATO AND YOGURT PIZZA

Serves 1.

10 ounces Basic Pizza Dough (page 28)

4 ounces low-moisture part-skim mozzarella cheese, diced

4 ripe plum tomatoes, sliced

2 to 3 tablespoons yellow cornmeal

2 tablespoons Fresh Basil Pesto (page 22)

1/4 cup nonfat yogurt

Place an ovenstone on the lowest rack of the oven, closest to the heating element. Preheat at 500 degrees F. for 1 hour.

Roll the pizza dough into a circle 9 inches in diameter. Spread the cornmeal on the pizza peel just in the area where the pizza will lie. Place the dough on top of the cornmeal. Spread the mozzarella on the dough, then top with tomato slices. Slide the pizza onto the preheated ovenstone and bake at 500 degrees F. for 10 to 14 minutes until the crust is golden.

While the pizza is baking, combine the pesto and the yogurt. Set the mixture aside. Remove the pizza from the oven and place it on a cooling rack. Brush the top with the pesto-yogurt mixture and let the pizza cool about 5 minutes. Cut into slices with a pizza wheel and serve.

Page 30: Top, Pesto and Vegetable Pleated Whole Wheat Pizza; Bottom, Caribbean Salad Pizza. Page 31: Top, Three Color Pepper Pizza; Bottom Right, Ham and Gorgonzola Calzone, Bottom Left, Veggie and Fruit Calzone.

PESTO AND VEGETABLE PLEATED WHOLE WHEAT PIZZA

Serves 1.

10 ounces Whole Wheat Pizza Dough (page 18)

2 to 3 tablespoons yellow cornmeal

3 tablespoons Fresh Basil Pesto (page 22)

2 ounces low-moisture part-skim mozzarella cheese, diced

1 small red onion, very thinly sliced

4 water-packed artichoke hearts, drained and quartered

4 ripe plum tomatoes, very thinly sliced

Olive oil for brushing

2 tablespoons freshly grated Romano or Parmesan cheese, plus extra for garnish

Place an ovenstone on the lowest rack of the oven, closest to the heating element. Preheat at 500 degrees F. for 1 hour.

Roll the pizza dough into a circle 9 inches in diameter. Spread the cornmeal on the pizza peel just in the area where the pizza will lie. Place the dough on top of the cornmeal. Brush the dough with pesto from one edge of the pizza to the other. Sprinkle the mozzarella on the pesto, then arrange the onion, artichoke and tomato slices on the entire surface of the dough. Top with 2 tablespoons of Romano or Parmesan cheese, then fold the edge of the dough into the center of the pizza, pleating the dough as you fold; leave an open area about 3 inches in diameter in the center of the pizza.

Slide the pizza onto the preheated ovenstone and bake at 500 degrees F. for 10 to 14 minutes until the crust is golden. Remove the pizza from the oven and place it on a cooling rack. Brush the top with olive oil and dust with Romano or Parmesan cheese. Cut into slices with a pizza wheel and serve.

GRILLED PIZZAS

" I've devoted my life to trying to give people the confidence to make their own pizza at home. But if you don't have the inclination to make pizza dough from scratch, there are plenty of bakeries out there that will sell or give you a piece of dough, which is the next best thing to making your own."

Serves 1.

12 ounces Basic Pizza Dough (page 28)

Olive oil for brushing

2 tablespoons Fresh Basil Pesto (page 22)

4 ounces Bel Paese cheese, sliced

12 oil-packed sun-dried tomatoes, drained

2 tablespoons thick tomato sauce

4 ounces low-moisture part-skim mozzarella cheese, diced

12 black olives, pitted and halved

Freshly grated Romano cheese for garnish

Preheat a grill or outdoor barbecue.

Divide the pizza dough in half and roll each half into a 6-inch circle. Brush the pizzas with olive oil, then place them, oiled side down, on a hot grill. Cook the pizzas until the dough firms up and the first side is scored with grill marks; watch the pizzas carefully so that they don't burn. Brush the other side with olive oil, then turn the pizzas.

Brush pesto on one of the pizzas and top with Bel Paese and sun-dried tomatoes. Spread tomato sauce on the other pizza, then add mozzarella and black olives.

Remove the pizzas from the grill and place them on serving plates. Brush the edges with olive oil, dust with Romano cheese and serve.

JUST PESTO PIZZA

Serves 1.

1/4 cup pine nuts

10 ounces Basic Pizza Dough (page 28)

2 to 3 tablespoons yellow cornmeal

1/4 cup Fresh Basil Pesto (page 22)

4 ounces low-moisture, part-skim mozzarella cheese, diced

Place an ovenstone on the lowest rack of the oven, closest to the heating element. Preheat at 500 degrees F. for 1 hour.

Place the pine nuts in a dry skillet and roast over low heat until lightly browned; shake the pan or stir frequently and watch carefully so they don't burn. Set the roasted pine nuts aside.

Roll the pizza dough into a 9-inch circle. Sprinkle the cornmeal on the pizza peel just in the area where the pizza will lie. Place the dough on top of the cornmeal. Brush the pesto on the dough, then add the mozzarella.

Slide the pizza onto the preheated ovenstone and bake at 500 degrees F. for 5 to 8 minutes until the crust is golden. Remove the pizza from the oven and place on a cooling rack. Garnish with roasted pine nuts, cut into slices with a pizza wheel and serve.

JUST PARMESAN PIZZA

Serves 1.

10 ounces Basic Pizza Dough (page 28)

2 to 3 tablespoons yellow cornmeal

2 tablespoons olive oil

1/4 cup freshly grated Parmesan cheese

Place an ovenstone on the lowest rack of the oven, closest to the heating element. Preheat at 500 degrees F. for 1 hour.

Roll the pizza dough into a 9-inch circle, being careful not to fold, crease or perforate the dough, or the dough will not puff. Sprinkle the cornmeal on the pizza peel just in the area where the pizza will lie. Place the dough on top of the cornmeal.

Slide the pizza onto the preheated ovenstone and bake at 500 degrees F. for 5 to 8 minutes. As it bakes the dough will fill with air and puff up like pita bread.

Remove the pizza from the oven and place on a cooling rack. Brush the pizza with olive oil, then sprinkle on the Parmesan. Cut into slices with a pizza wheel and serve.

LOW-FAT MIXED MUSHROOM PIZZA

Serves 1.

1 tablespoon olive oil, plus extra for brushing

1 pound mixed mushrooms
(such as button, oyster, shiitake, portabella, chanterelle, cepes or enoki)

Salt and freshly ground black pepper

10 ounces Basic Pizza Dough (page 28)

2 to 3 tablespoons yellow cornmeal

4 ounces low-moisture, part-skim mozzarella cheese, diced

1 small red onion, thinly sliced

1 ripe plum tomato, thinly sliced

Freshly grated Romano cheese for garnish

Place an ovenstone on the lowest rack of the oven, closest to the heating element. Preheat at 500 degrees F. for 1 hour.

Heat 1 tablespoon olive oil in a sauté pan, then add the mushrooms. Season with salt and pepper to taste and cook for 3 to 5 minutes over medium heat until soft. Remove the mushrooms from the heat and let them cool slightly.

Roll the pizza dough into a 9-inch circle. Sprinkle the cornmeal on the pizza peel just in the area where the pizza will lie. Place the dough on top of the cornmeal. Spread the mozzarella on the dough, then top with the mushrooms, onion and tomato.

Slide the pizza onto the preheated ovenstone and bake at 500 degrees F. for 10 to 14 minutes. Remove the pizza from the oven and place it on a cooling rack. Brush the edge with olive oil, sprinkle with Romano cheese and serve.

PRIMAVERA PIZZA

Serves 1.

10 ounces Basic Pizza Dough (page 28)

2 to 3 tablespoons yellow cornmeal

4 ounces low-moisture, part-skim mozzarella cheese, diced

2 small plum tomatoes, sliced

1 small zucchini, sliced

1/2 cup sliced button mushrooms

1 small onion, sliced

2 teaspoons chopped fresh basil

Salt and freshly ground black pepper

Olive oil for brushing

Freshly grated Romano cheese for garnish

Place an ovenstone on the lowest rack of the oven, closest to the heating element. Preheat at 500 degrees F. for 1 hour.

Roll the pizza dough into a 9-inch circle. Sprinkle the cornmeal on the pizza peel just in the area where the pizza will lie. Place the dough on top of the cornmeal. Spread the mozzarella on the dough, then top with the vegetables. Sprinkle with basil and season with salt and pepper to taste. Slide the pizza onto the preheated ovenstone and bake at 500 degrees F. for 10 to 14 minutes until the crust is golden.

Remove the pizza from the oven and place it on a cooling rack. Brush the edge with olive oil and dust with Romano cheese. Cut into slices and serve.

CARIBBEAN SALAD PIZZA

Serves 4 to 6.

19 ounces Basic Pizza Dough (page 28)

2 to 3 tablespoons yellow cornmeal

Olive oil for brushing

Freshly ground black pepper

4 ounces Fontinella cheese, diced (sharp white cheddar can be substituted)

10 ounces low-moisture part-skim mozzarella cheese, diced

4 cups mixed salad greens (such as Boston bibb, butternut, romaine or dandelion)

1 cup diced papaya

1 small Vidalia or red onion, grilled and sliced

1 large orange, peeled, seeded and sliced

1/2 cup shredded coconut

1 small roasted red bell pepper (page 23), julienned

2 tablespoons balsamic vinegar

1/3 cup olive oil

Juice of 2 limes

Place an ovenstone on the lowest rack of the oven, closest to the heating element. Preheat at 500 degrees F. for 1 hour.

Roll the pizza dough into a 14-inch circle. Sprinkle the cornmeal on the pizza peel just in the area where the pizza will lie. Place the dough on top of the cornmeal. Brush the dough with olive oil and season it with freshly ground black pepper. Top with the Fontinella and mozzarella cheese. Slide the pizza onto the preheated ovenstone and bake at 500 degrees F. for 10 to 14 minutes, until the crust is golden.

While the pizza is baking, prepare the salad. Wash the greens and dry them in a salad spinner or colander. Place the greens in a bowl and add the papaya, onion, orange, coconut and roasted pepper. In a small bowl, whisk together the vinegar, 1/3 cup olive oil and lime juice. Pour the vinaigrette over the salad and toss.

Remove the pizza from the oven and place it on a cooling rack. Top the pizza with the salad, then brush the edge with olive oil. Sprinkle with black pepper, slice and serve.

39

GOAT CHEESE AND VEGETABLE PIZZA

Serves 2.

14 ounces Basic Pizza Dough (page 28)

2 to 3 tablespoons yellow cornmeal

Olive oil for brushing

4 ounces low-moisture part-skim mozzarella cheese, diced

12 sun-dried oil-packed tomatoes, drained and cut into strips

4 water-packed artichoke hearts, drained and quartered

1 small roasted green bell pepper (page 23), cut into strips

4 ounces goat cheese, cubed

4 bacon strips, cooked until crisp

12 fresh basil leaves, cut into strips

Freshly grated Parmesan cheese for garnish

Place an ovenstone on the lowest rack of the oven, closest to the heating element. Preheat at 500 degrees F. for 1 hour.

Roll the pizza dough into a 14-inch circle. Spread the cornmeal on the pizza peel just in the area where the pizza will lie. Place the dough on top of the cornmeal. Brush with dough with olive oil and top with mozzarella cheese. Arrange the sun-dried tomatoes, artichoke hearts and bell pepper on top of the mozzarella. Scatter the chunks of goat cheese on top of the vegetables, then crumble the bacon over the pizza.

Slide the pizza onto the preheated ovenstone and bake at 500 degrees F. for 8 to 10 minutes until the crust is golden. Remove pizza from the oven and place it on a cooling rack. Sprinkle fresh basil leaves over the pizza and garnish with Parmesan cheese.

TAPENADE PIZZA

Serves 1.

1 pound pitted Greek Kalamata olives

4 anchovy fillets

2 tablespoons drained capers

1/4 cup olive oil

Juice of 1/2 lemon

2 ounces Romano cheese, grated

10 ounces Basic Pizza Dough (page 28)

2 to 3 tablespoons yellow cornmeal

Place an ovenstone on the lowest rack of the oven, closest to the heating element. Preheat at 500 degrees F. for 1 hour.

Combine the olives, anchovies, capers, olive oil, lemon juice and half (1 ounce) of the grated Romano cheese in a food processor. Purée the mixture until it has the consistency of a paste.

Roll the pizza dough into a 9-inch circle. Spread the cornmeal on a pizza peel just in the area where the pizza will lie. Place the dough on top of the cornmeal. Spread the olive paste on the dough.

Slide the pizza onto the preheated ovenstone and bake at 500 degrees F. for 5 to 8 minutes. Remove the pizza from the oven and transfer it to a cooling rack. Garnish with the remaining grated Romano cheese and serve.

PIZZA WITH ROASTED PEPPERS, CAPERS AND A GARLIC-FLAVORED CRUST

Serves 4.

1 large red bell pepper

1 large yellow bell pepper

10 ounces Basic Pizza Dough (page 28)

2 to 3 tablespoons yellow cornmeal

Olive oil for brushing

2 garlic cloves, minced

1/4 cup drained capers

2 tablespoons freshly grated Romano cheese

" Tomato sauce is on its way out as the main underlying flavor for pizza. Once you eliminate that acidy tomato taste, you can go anywhere you want with pizza."

Roast the bell peppers over an open flame or in an oven broiler, turning them frequently. When the skin is charred on all sides, plunge the peppers into ice water. Scrape and pull away the blackened peel, then slice the flesh of the peppers into long, narrow strips.

Place an ovenstone on the lowest rack of the oven, closest to the heating element. Preheat at 500 degrees F. for 1 hour.

Roll the pizza dough into a rectangle, approximately 5 1/2 by 15-inches. Spread the cornmeal on a pizza peel just in the area where the dough will lie. Place the dough on top of the cornmeal and brush it with olive oil. Press the minced garlic into the dough.

Starting at one end of the rectangle, alternate strips of red and yellow peppers, covering the surface of the dough. Sprinkle capers on top of the peppers, then score the edge of the dough with a knife (this will create a scalloped edge when the pizza is baked).

Slide the pizza onto the preheated ovenstone and bake at 500 degrees for 8 to 10 minutes until the crust is golden. Transfer the baked pizza to a rack and brush the edge with olive oil. Sprinkle with Romano cheese, slice and serve.

THREE COLOR PEPPER PIZZA

Serves 4 to 6.

2 tablespoons olive oil, plus extra for brushing

4 garlic cloves, minced

1 ripe plum tomato, seeded and chopped

1 roasted green bell pepper (page 23), sliced

1 roasted red bell pepper (page 23), sliced

1 roasted yellow bell pepper (page 23), sliced

19 ounces Basic Pizza Dough (page 28)

2 to 3 tablespoons yellow cornmeal

8 ounces low-moisture part skim mozzarella cheese, diced

Freshly grated Romano cheese for garnish

Place an ovenstone on the lowest rack of the oven, closest to the heating element. Preheat at 500 degrees F. for 1 hour.

Heat the olive oil in a large skillet, then add the garlic, tomatoes and roasted peppers. Cook the mixture over medium heat for 10 to 15 minutes to soften the tomatoes.

Roll the pizza dough into a rectangle slightly smaller than the pizza stone. Spread the cornmeal on a pizza peel just in the area where the pizza will lie. Place the dough on top of the cornmeal, then spread with the mozzarella. Spoon the pepper-tomato mixture on the pizza. Slide the pizza onto the preheated ovenstone and bake at 500 degrees F. for 10 to 14 minutes. Remove the pizza from the oven and transfer it to a cooling rack. Brush the edges with olive oil, dust the top with Romano cheese, then serve.

MINI SHRIMP, CHICKEN AND PORK CALZONE WITH TWO DIPPING SAUCES

Makes 20 to 24 mini calzone.

2 tablespoons olive oil

4 ounces each pork and chicken, diced

4 ounces shrimp, peeled, deveined and diced

Salt and freshly ground black pepper

1 1/2 cups bean sprouts

4 green onions, diced

8 water chestnuts, diced

1/4 teaspoon diced ginger

1 1/2 teaspoons soy sauce

2 tablespoons dry sherry

19 ounces Basic Pizza Dough (page 28)

Sweet and Sour Sauce for dipping (recipe follows)

Apricot Sauce for dipping (recipe follows)

Preheat an ovenstone on the center rack of the oven for 30 minutes at 500 degrees F. Heat the olive oil in a large skillet and cook the pork and chicken. Add the shrimp and season the mixture with salt and pepper. Cook briefly, until the shrimp pieces turn pink, then remove the shrimp, pork, and chicken from the pan and set them aside.

To the hot pan, add the bean sprouts, green onions, water chestnuts and ginger. When the ingredients are hot, return the pork and shrimp to the pan. Add the soy sauce and sherry; reduce over medium high heat. Transfer the filling mixture to a colander and let drain while shaping the pizza dough.

Roll the pizza dough into a sheet about 1/4-inch thick. Cut circles of dough with a 2-inch biscuit cutter.

Place a spoonful of filling on the center of each circle and seal the calzone following the instructions on page 29. Place the calzone on a baking sheet lined with parchment paper. Bake on the preheated ovenstone for 10 to 15 minutes at 500 degrees F. until golden brown. Remove the calzone from the oven and transfer them to a cooling rack. Serve with Sweet and Sour Sauce and/or Apricot Sauce.

SWEET AND SOUR SAUCE

1/2 cup sugar

2 tablespoons soy sauce

3 tablespoons dry sherry

3 tablespoons thick tomato sauce

1/2 cup orange juice

2 tablespoons cornstarch

Combine all of the ingredients, except the cornstarch, in a small saucepan. Bring the mixture to a boil, then reduce the heat and simmer the sauce for 10 to 15 minutes, stirring frequently. Pour 1/4 cup of the sauce into a small bowl and stir in the cornstarch. When smooth, add the cornstarch mixture to the sauce in the pan and stir until thickened. Chill before serving.

APRICOT SAUCE

1/4 cup dried apricots

3/4 cup sugar

1/8 teaspoon cayenne pepper

Salt to taste

1/2 cup orange juice

Place the apricots in a small bowl and add hot water to cover. Soak until soft, then drain.

In a heavy saucepan, combine the apricots, sugar, cayenne, salt and orange juice. Bring the mixture to a boil, then reduce the heat and simmer for 15 to 20 minutes, stirring frequently, until the sauce thickens. Chill and serve.

"When making calzone your filling needs to be more dry than wet. Use your hands to combine the ingredients but be sure to keep your hands clean while sealing the calzone so the edges of the dough stay dry and stick together."

SHRIMP AND BACON CALZONE

Makes 8 to 10 calzone.

12 large shrimp, peeled and deveined

12 bacon strips, cooked until crisp

28 ounces canned whole tomatoes, drained

2 garlic cloves, minced

6 ounces low-moisture part-skim mozzarella cheese, diced

4 ounces Fontinella cheese, diced (sharp white Cheddar can be substituted)

19 ounces Basic Pizza Dough (page 28)

Freshly grated Romano cheese for garnish

Preheat an ovenstone on the center rack of the oven for 30 minutes at 500 degrees F. Boil the shrimp until firm and pink. Chop the shrimp and place the pieces in a medium bowl; crumble in the bacon. Dice the tomatoes and blot dry with paper towels. Add the tomatoes to the shrimp mixture, then fold in the garlic, mozzarella and Fontinella. Set the shrimp filling aside while shaping the dough.

Roll the pizza dough into a sheet about 1/4-inch thick. Cut circles of dough with a 4-inch biscuit cutter. Place a heaping tablespoon of shrimp filling on the center of each circle and seal the calzone following the instructions on page 29.

Place the calzone on a baking sheet lined with parchment paper. Bake on the preheated ovenstone for 10 to 15 minutes at 500 degrees F. until golden brown. Remove the calzone from the oven and transfer to a cooling rack. Sprinkle with Romano cheese and let cool about 5 minutes before serving.

My Basic Pizza Dough can also be made in a bread machine. Follow manufacturers instructions on measurements for water, yeast, and flour. Don't forget to add the salt and olive oil. Mix and let rise once. Remove pizza dough from machine and place in floured, covered bowl. Let rise 2 to 3 more hours then it's ready to use.

HAM AND GORGONZOLA CALZONE

Makes 8 to 10 calzone.

10 ounces ricotta cheese

6 ounces low-moisture part-skim mozzarella cheese, diced

4 ounces Gorgonzola cheese, crumbled

4 ounces Romano cheese, grated

8 ounces ham, diced

12 Italian parsley leaves, minced

28 ounces canned plum tomatoes, drained

1/4 teaspoon dried rosemary

19 ounces Basic Pizza Dough (page 28)

Freshly grated Romano cheese for garnish

Preheat an ovenstone on the center rack of the oven for 30 minutes at 500 degrees F.

In a large bowl, combine the cheeses, ham and parsley. Dice the tomatoes and blot dry on paper towels. Add the tomatoes and rosemary to the bowl and stir until the ingredients are well blended. Set the ham and cheese filling mixture aside while shaping the dough.

Roll the pizza dough into a sheet about 1/4-inch thick. Cut circles of dough with a 4-inch biscuit cutter.

Place a heaping tablespoon of ham and cheese filling on the center of each circle and seal the calzone following the instructions on page 29. Place the calzone on a baking sheet lined with parchment paper. Bake on the preheated ovenstone for 10 to 15 minutes at 500 degrees F. until golden brown. Remove the calzone from the oven and transfer to a cooling rack. Sprinkle with Romano cheese and let cool about 5 minutes before serving.

PASTA AND SOUPS

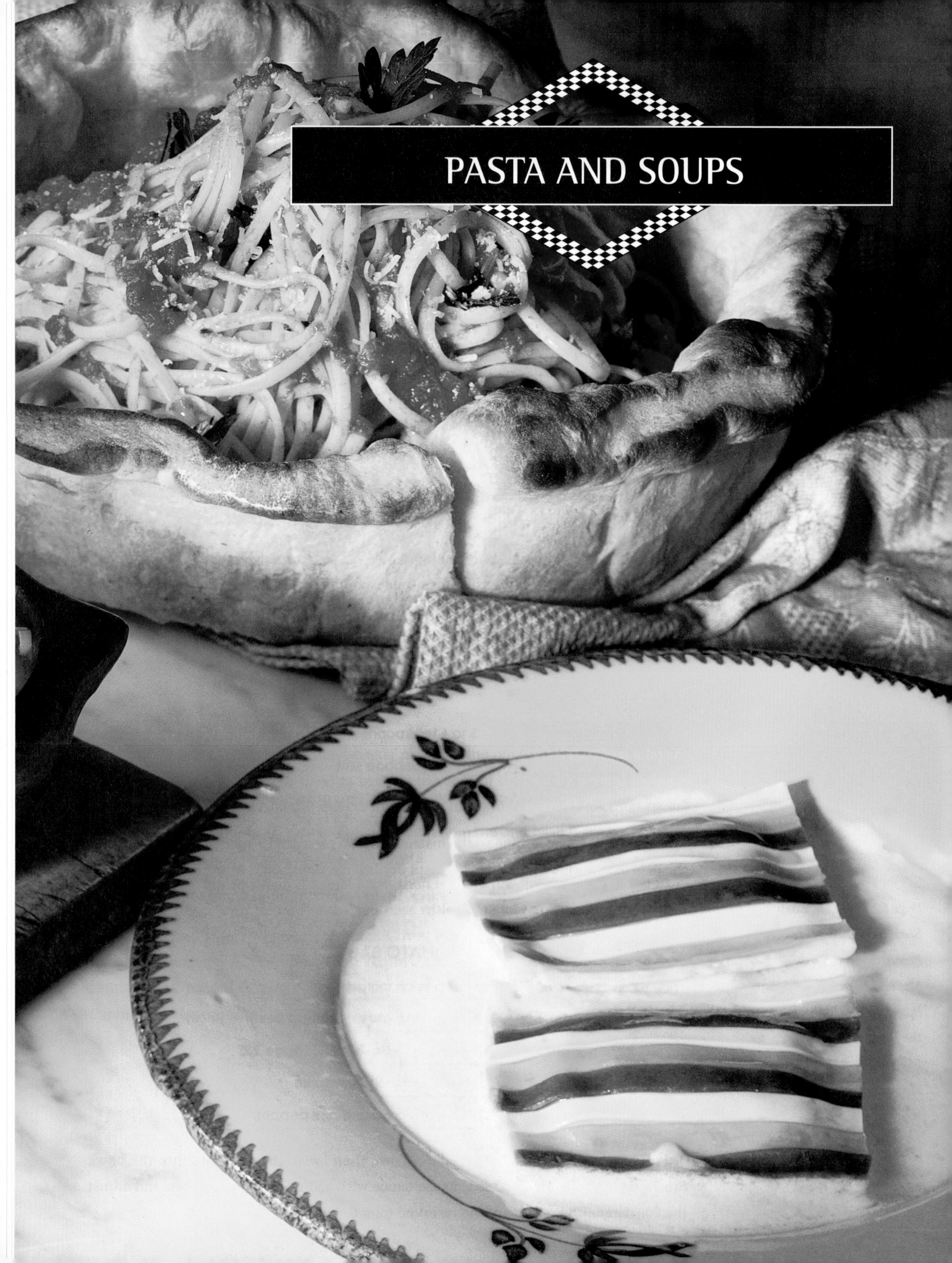

STUFFED PASTA SHELLS

Serves 6.

Olive oil for brushing

8 ounces low-moisture part-skim mozzarella cheese, diced

15 ounces ricotta cheese

4 ounces Fontinella cheese, diced (sharp white Cheddar can be substituted)

12 ounces broccoli florets or spinach, chopped

1/8 teaspoon nutmeg

1/4 teaspoon dried marjoram

1/4 teaspoon dried basil

2 garlic cloves, minced

16 jumbo pasta shells, cooked and drained

1 cup seasoned bread crumbs

Fresh parsley leaves for garnish

"Baked pasta must rest for about 15 minutes after leaving the hot oven so that it has the chance to set and firm up."

Preheat the oven to 375 degrees F. Brush bottom and sides of a 9 by 12-inch baking dish with olive oil.

In a mixing bowl, combine the ricotta, 5 ounces of the mozzarella, Fontinella, broccoli or spinach, nutmeg, marjoram, basil and garlic. Stuff the pasta shells with the ricotta filling and place them side by side in the baking pan. Sprinkle bread crumbs and the remaining 3 ounces of mozzarella cheese over the stuffed pasta shells, then cover the pan with aluminum foil. Bake for 20 minutes; remove the foil for the last 5 minutes of baking. Remove the stuffed shells from the oven and let them cool briefly. Garnish with parsley leaves and serve.

PASTA IN THE DOUGH

Serves 4.

12 ounces Basic Pizza Dough (page 28)

2 tablespoons olive oil

2 garlic cloves, chopped

1 medium onion, diced

1 cup thick tomato sauce

6 water-packed artichoke hearts, drained and chopped

1 pound dried spaghetti pasta

4 ounces low-moisture part-skim mozzarella cheese, diced

2 tablespoons freshly grated Romano cheese for garnish

Preheat the oven to 425 degrees F.

Roll the dough into a circle approximately 12 inches in diameter, then press it into a 10-inch round deep-dish pizza pan. Oil a large sheet of aluminum foil and place it over the dough. Pour 1 pound of dried beans on top of the foil to maintain the shape of the dough as it bakes. Place the pan in the hot oven and bake for 12 to 14 minutes, until the edge is golden brown. Transfer the baked dough to a cooling rack; remove the foil and dried beans. Reserve the pizza dough shell for assembly.

Heat the olive oil in a large skillet and sauté the garlic and onion until tender. Add the tomato sauce and artichokes, then reduce the heat and simmer the mixture for 5 minutes until warmed through. Cook the spaghetti in a large pot of boiling salted water until al dente. Drain the pasta and add it to the skillet. Toss the noodles in the tomato sauce mixture.

Spoon the spaghetti and sauce into the baked shell, then top with the mozzarella. Return the pan to the hot oven and bake for 10 minutes to melt the cheese. Remove the pasta from the oven, then dust it with Romano cheese. Using a spatula, lift the filled shell out of the pan. Cut the dough into wedges and serve.

PENNE PASTA WITH SPICY SAUCE

Serves 4.

1 ripe plum tomato

3 tablespoons olive oil

1 small hot red chili (such as Thai), seeded and cut into 4 strips

1 medium onion, diced

4 garlic cloves, sliced

8 ounces pancetta, diced (bacon can be substituted)

1 pound penne pasta

12 fresh basil leaves, coarsely chopped

1/4 cup freshly grated Romano cheese

"Allow 4 ounces of pasta per person and throw it into the boiling salted water all at once. Stir well to prevent the pasta from settling on the bottom of the pot and sticking."

Bring 2 cups of water to a boil in a medium saucepan. Immerse the plum tomato in the boiling water until the skin cracks, then plunge it into cold water. Remove the skin from the tomato, then dice the flesh.

Heat the olive oil in a skillet and add the diced tomato, red chili, onion, garlic and pancetta. Sauté the ingredients until the onion is translucent, then remove and discard the chili strips.

Cook the penne pasta in a large pot of boiling salted water until al dente. Drain the pasta and place the noodles in a serving bowl. Pour the spicy sauce over the pasta and top with basil leaves and Romano cheese. Serve immediately.

LINGUINE FROM HELL

Serves 4.

1 pound linguine

1/4 cup olive oil

1 pound large shrimp, peeled and deveined

2 garlic cloves, minced

1/4 cup fresh lime juice

1 teaspoon Jamaican hot sauce

1 teaspoon jalapeño pepper sauce

1 tablespoon dark rum

Italian flat-leaf parsley for garnish

Cook the linguine in a large pot of boiling salted water until al dente. Drain and set aside.

Heat the olive oil in a large skillet and add the shrimp and garlic. Cook the shrimp for several minutes over medium high heat until cooked through, then stir in the lime juice, Jamaican hot sauce, jalapeño pepper sauce and rum; if the rum ignites, stir the mixture until the flames subside.

Add the linguine to the skillet and toss the pasta lightly in the sauce. Pour the contents of the skillet into a large serving bowl, garnish with Italian parsley leaves and serve.

FARFALLE WITH CASHEW GINGER SAUCE

Serves 6.

1 3/4 cups whole raw cashews

4 tablespoons olive oil

1 teaspoon chopped fresh ginger root

1 teaspoon diced jalapeño pepper

1 1/2 pounds farfalle pasta

2 tablespoons chopped green onion tops for garnish

Place 1/2 cup of the cashews in a food processor along with 1 tablespoon olive oil. Process the mixture into a paste and set it aside. Roast 1 cup of the cashews for 2 to 3 minutes in a dry skillet over medium heat, shaking the pan frequently until the cashews are lightly browned. Set the roasted cashews aside. Chop the remaining 1/4 cup of cashews and reserve as a garnish.

Heat the remaining 3 tablespoons of olive oil in a large skillet and sauté the ginger and jalapeño pepper until tender. Remove the mixture from the heat and stir in the cashew paste and roasted cashews.

Cook the farfalle pasta in a large pot of boiling salted water until al dente. Drain the pasta and add it to the skillet. Toss the noodles in the cashew mixture, then transfer the farfalle to a serving platter. Garnish with green onions and chopped cashews, then serve.

STIR-FRIED SEAFOOD ON PASTA SQUARES

Serves 6.

2 tablespoons vegetable oil

1 garlic clove, minced

1 teaspoon minced fresh ginger root

1 teaspoon curry powder

10 large shrimp, peeled, deveined and cooked

1 lobster tail, cooked and coarsely chopped

24 parboiled crawfish tails

1 pound asparagus tips, cooked until tender

3 ripe plum tomatoes, diced

1/2 cup chicken stock

1/4 cup plain lowfat yogurt

4 thin sheets of fresh pasta, approximately 6 by 12-inches each

4 green onions, diced

Heat the oil in a large skillet and sauté the garlic and ginger briefly. Stir in the curry powder, then add the seafood. Stir-fry the ingredients over fairly high heat for 2 to 3 minutes. Add the asparagus, tomatoes and chicken stock, then sauté the mixture an additional 2 minutes. Remove the pan from the heat and stir in the yogurt.

Cut the pasta into 2-inch squares and cook it in a large pot of boiling salted water until al dente. Drain the pasta, then place it on a serving platter and pour the stir-fry mixture over the top. Garnish with green onions and serve immediately.

EASY SHRIMP AND ANGEL HAIR PASTA

Serves 6.

2 pounds ripe tomatoes

3 tablespoons olive oil

1 1/2 pounds large shrimp, peeled and deveined

4 garlic cloves, diced

2 pounds angel hair pasta

1 teaspoon crushed red pepper flakes

Salt and freshly ground black pepper

"Don't worry if you have a little water left after you drain the pasta. The liquid will blend in with the sauce and seasonings in your serving bowl."

Dice the tomatoes, reserving 1/2 cup of the dice for use later in the dish.

Heat the olive oil in a large skillet and add the bulk of the diced tomato along with the shrimp and garlic. Cook the mixture over medium high heat for several minutes until the shrimp turn pink and are cooked through. Remove the shrimp from the pan and set them aside.

Purée the tomato and garlic mixture in a blender, food processor or food mill, then return the mixture to the skillet. Fold the shrimp and the remaining 1/2 cup diced tomatoes into the purée. Simmer uncovered for 2 to 3 minutes, stirring frequently.

Cook the angel hair pasta in a large pot of boiling salted water until al dente. Drain the noodles and place them in a large serving bowl. Pour the shrimp and sauce over the pasta and toss. Add the red pepper flakes, then season to taste with salt and pepper. Serve immediately.

ROTELLE WITH BELL PEPPERS

Serves 4.

2 red bell peppers

2 yellow bell peppers

2 green bell peppers

1/2 cup olive oil

1/2 teaspoon crushed red pepper flakes

Salt and freshly ground black pepper

1 pound rotelle pasta

4 ounces Fontinella cheese, grated (sharp white Cheddar can be substituted)

Roast the bell peppers according to the instructions on page 23. Remove the skin from the bell peppers and slice the flesh into thin strips. Heat the olive oil in a skillet and sauté the bell pepper strips for 3 to 4 minutes. Stir in the red pepper flakes, then season the mixture with salt and pepper.

Cook the rotelle pasta in a large pot of boiling water until al dente. Drain the rotelle and place the pasta on a large serving platter. Top the pasta with the bell pepper mixture, sprinkle with grated Fontinella cheese and serve.

MEXICAN BLACK BEAN SOUP

Serves 4.

1/4 cup olive oil

6 garlic cloves, chopped

2 large yellow onions, diced

1 pound chorizo sausage, diced

6 cups chicken stock

1 pound dried black beans

2 tablespoons ground cumin

2 tablespoons dried oregano

2 tablespoons dried thyme

1 teaspoon minced jalapeño

Sour cream for garnish

1 ripe tomato, diced, for garnish

1 green onion, diced, for garnish

Heat the oil in a large pot and sauté the garlic and onions with the chorizo. Add the stock and beans. Stir in the cumin, oregano, thyme and jalapeño. Lower the heat and simmer for 1 to 2 hours until the beans are tender and the soup begins to thicken.

Purée half of the soup in a food processor. Stir the purée into the soup, then cook for a few minutes to heat it through. Pour black bean soup into individual serving bowls and garnish with a dollop of sour cream and a sprinkling of diced tomato and green onion.

PASTA E FAGIOLI (PASTA AND BEAN SOUP)

Serves 4.

1 pound dried white kidney beans

1/3 cup olive oil

1 medium onion, diced

1 carrot, diced

1 celery stalk, diced

6 cups chicken stock

8 ounces bacon, cooked until crisp and then crumbled

12 ounces cooked short tubular pasta (such as ditalini or cannolicchi)

Salt and freshly ground black pepper

1/2 cup freshly grated Parmesan cheese for garnish

Soak the beans overnight in cold water. The next day, drain the beans and cook them until tender. Purée half of the beans in a food processor and set aside. Leave the remaining beans whole.

Heat the oil in a stockpot and sauté the onion, carrot and celery until tender. Add the chicken stock and puréed beans. Bring the soup to a boil, then reduce the heat and simmer for 20 minutes. Stir in the whole beans, crumbled bacon and pasta. Season to taste with salt and pepper. Ladle the soup into bowls, then garnish with Parmesan cheese and serve.

TUSCAN TOMATO SOUP

Serves 4.

1/4 cup olive oil

6 carrots, diced

6 celery stalks, with tops, diced

2 medium yellow onions, diced

2 28-ounce cans plum tomatoes, with juice

1/4 cup (1/2 stick) butter

Salt and freshly ground black pepper

12 fresh basil leaves

1/4 cup Italian flat-leaf parsley

Heat the olive oil in a large, heavy stockpot and sauté the carrots, celery and onions over high heat until tender. Stir in the tomatoes and butter. Reduce the heat to low and simmer for 25 to 30 minutes. Season with salt and pepper to taste. Just before serving, add the basil and parsley. Cook an additional five minutes, then spoon into bowls.

WHAT A GREAT NORTHERN BEAN IT IS!

Serves 6.

2 pounds dried Great Northern white beans

1/2 cup olive oil

8 garlic cloves, chopped

2 medium white onions, diced

2 medium red bell peppers, seeded and diced

6 ounces sweet Italian sausage

6 ounces hot Italian sausage

2 quarts chicken stock

1 ham bone (optional)

2 tablespoons Fresh Basil Pesto (page 22)

1 tablespoon salt (use more or less according to taste)

1 tablespoon black pepper (use more or less according to taste)

1/2 cup loosely packed Italian flat-leaf parsley for garnish

Soak the white beans overnight in cold water. The next day, drain the beans and place them in a large saucepan. Add water to cover and bring the beans to a boil over high heat. Reduce the heat to low and simmer for 20 minutes until the beans are tender. Drain the beans and set them aside.

Heat the olive oil in a large skillet, then sauté the garlic, onions and red bell peppers until tender. Cook the Italian sausage on top of the stove or in a microwave until the juices run clear. Drain the oil from the sausage, then remove the casings and crumble the meat.

In a 6-quart stockpot, combine the cooked vegetables, the Italian sausage, chicken stock, beans and ham bone, if used. Simmer the soup for 40 minutes. Remove the soup from the heat and stir in the pesto. Season to taste with salt and pepper, garnish with Italian flat-leaf parsley, then serve.

SALADS AND BREADS

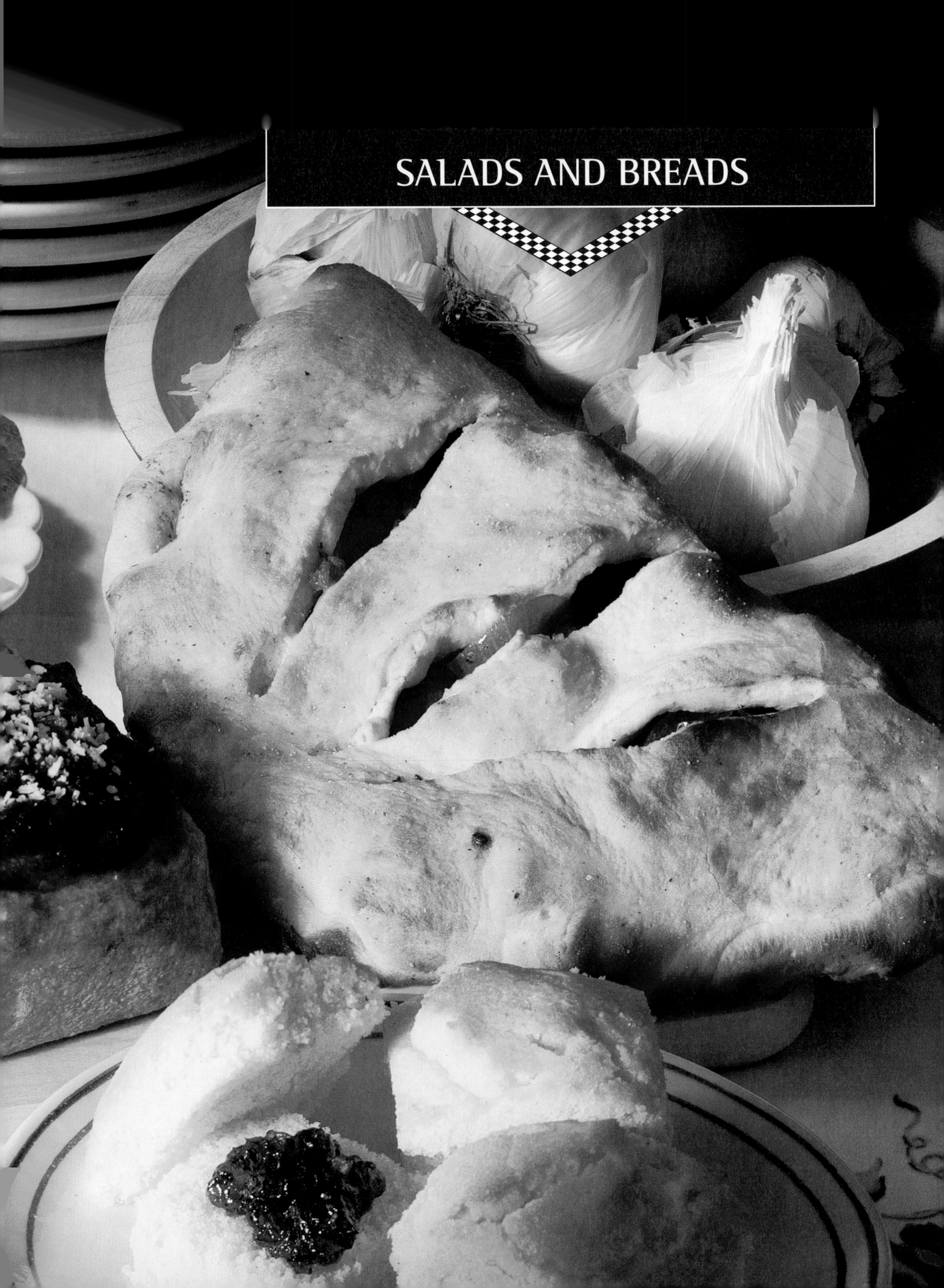

WILD GREENS SALAD WITH HONEY MUSTARD, GARLIC AND GORGONZOLA DRESSING

Serves 4.

1 tablespoon honey mustard

1 garlic clove, minced

1/2 cup olive oil

2 tablespoons red wine vinegar

Salt and freshly ground black pepper

1 pound mixed salad greens (use a combination of romaine, escarole, butternut, arugula, Boston bibb or red tip leaf lettuce)

3 ounces Gorgonzola cheese

Italian flat-leaf parsley and crumbled crisp-cooked bacon for garnish

In a medium bowl, combine the honey mustard, garlic, olive oil and vinegar. Whisk the ingredients, then season to taste with salt and pepper. Set the dressing aside.

Wash and dry the greens, then cut the leaves into bite-sized pieces. Arrange the cut greens on a large serving platter. Pour the dressing over the greens and toss. Crumble the Gorgonzola over the salad, then garnish with Italian parsley and crumbled bacon.

Page 74: Top Left, Antipasto Salad; Bottom, Tomato Bread; Page 75: Top Right, Stuffed Foccacia; Bottom, Cornbread Squares with Jalapeño Jelly.

FIVE GREEN SALAD WITH RASPBERRY WALNUT VINAIGRETTE

Serves 4.

2 tablespoons raspberry vinegar

1 tablespoon walnut oil

6 tablespoons olive oil

1 tablespoon garlic-flavored honey mustard

1 pound mixed salad greens
(use a combination of dandelion, arugula, radicchio, butternut and red oak leaf lettuce)

Salt and freshly ground black pepper

1/4 chopped walnuts for garnish

Combine the raspberry vinegar, walnut oil, olive oil and honey mustard in a small bowl and whisk until well blended. Set the vinaigrette aside.

Wash the greens and cut the leaves into bite-sized pieces. Place the cut leaves in a salad spinner. Spin the greens dry, then transfer them to a large bowl. Pour the dressing over the greens and toss until the leaves are coated. Season to taste with salt and pepper, garnish with chopped walnuts and serve.

ITALIAN SALAD

Serves 4.

1 portabella mushroom

1 small Vidalia or red onion

6 tablespoons olive oil, plus extra for brushing

2 tablespoons balsamic vinegar

2 garlic cloves, chopped

1 pound mixed salad greens
(use a combination of romaine, iceberg or red tip leaf lettuce)

1/2 cup reconstituted sun-dried tomatoes

1/4 cup Italian flat-leaf parsley

8 slices Romano cheese

"For safety's sake wild mushrooms need to be cooked longer than their cultivated cousins, so be sure to over — rather than undercook them."

Brush the mushroom and onion with olive oil and place them on a hot grill. Cook until tender, turning them frequently and brushing with additional oil as necessary. Remove the mushroom and onion from the grill and let cool. When cool enough to handle, julienne the portabella and cut the onion into thin slices, then set them aside.

Combine 6 tablespoons olive oil with the vinegar and chopped garlic in a small bowl; whisk the ingredients then set the dressing aside.

Wash the salad greens and chop the leaves into bite-sized pieces. Dry the cut leaves in a salad spinner or colander, then transfer them to a large bowl. Arrange the sun-dried tomatoes and parsley leaves on top of the salad and tuck slices of Romano among the leaves. Garnish with the mushroom and onion slices, toss lightly and serve.

MUSTARD VINAIGRETTE

Serves 2.

2 tablespoons sherry wine vinegar

6 tablespoons olive oil

1/2 teaspoon Dijon mustard

1/2 teaspoon minced fresh tarragon leaves

Salt and freshly ground black pepper to taste

Combine all of the ingredients in a small bowl and whisk until well blended. Chop assorted salad greens such as arugula, romaine, endive and red tip leaf lettuce into bite-sized pieces. Pour the dressing over the greens, toss and serve on chilled plates.

ANTIPASTO SALAD

Serves 10 to 12.

2 heads iceberg lettuce

1/4 cup Italian flat-leaf parsley, finely chopped

1 medium red onion, thinly sliced

8 ounces salami, thinly sliced and julienned

16 ounces canned chick peas (garbanzo beans), drained

2 medium lemons, halved

Antipasto Dressing (recipe follows)

6 to 8 romaine lettuce leaves

8 ounces pitted black olives, drained

2 medium ripe tomatoes, sliced into eighths

1 small (about 8 ounces) jar pepperoncini, drained

Freshly grated Romano cheese for garnish

"The secret to good antipasto is the delicious way lemon juice, fresh parsley and red onion combine with red wine vinaigrette for a really fresh-flavored salad."

Wash the iceberg lettuce, chop it into bite-sized pieces and place it in a salad spinner. Spin the lettuce dry, then transfer it to a large bowl. Add the parsley, onion, salami and chick peas. Squeeze the lemon juice onto the salad, then pour on the dressing. Toss lightly.

Wash and dry the romaine. Line a platter with the leaves and mound the tossed salad in the center. Make a well in the center of the mound and fill the indentation with olives. Ring the salad with tomato wedges and the remaining olives. Dot the salad with the pepperoncini. Sprinkle Romano cheese over the salad and serve immediately.

ANTIPASTO DRESSING

1/4 cup red wine vinegar

3/4 cup olive oil

1/2 teaspoon freshly ground black pepper

1 tablespoon freshly grated Romano cheese

2 garlic cloves, diced

In a small bowl, whisk together the vinegar and olive oil. Add the remaining ingredients and stir until well blended. Use the dressing immediately or store it up to a week at room temperature.

MAIN COURSE PIZZAS

TRADITIONAL DEEP-DISH PAN PIZZA

Serves 6.

1 tablespoon olive oil, plus extra for brushing

1 small onion, cut into rings

19 ounces Basic Pizza Dough (page 28)

1 tablespoon yellow cornmeal

6 ounces thick tomato sauce

2 tablespoons Fresh Basil Pesto (page 22)

10 ounces low-moisture part-skim mozzarella cheese, diced

8 ounces Italian sausage (page 24), cooked and sliced

4 ounces pepperoni, sliced

16 ounces canned plum tomatoes, drained and chopped

4 ripe plum tomatoes, sliced

3 garlic cloves, chopped

3 ounces smoked mozzarella cheese, diced

Freshly grated Romano cheese for sprinkling

Place an ovenstone on the lowest rack of the oven, closest to the heating element. Preheat at 500 degrees F. for 1 hour.

Heat 1 tablespoon olive oil in a small skillet and add the onion rings; cook over medium heat until tender and golden brown. Set the caramelized onions aside.

Brush a 14-inch deep-dish pizza pan with oil and spread the cornmeal on the bottom of the pan. Roll the pizza dough into a 16-inch circle and press it into the pan, forming a small lip up the side of the pan. Cover the pan with plastic wrap and let the dough rest about 5 minutes.

In a small bowl, combine the tomato sauce and pesto. Thin the mixture with a little water if the sauce seems too thick. Spoon the sauce onto the dough, then top with the low-moisture mozzarella. Shingle the Italian sausage, pepperoni, fresh and canned tomatoes, and caramelized onion on the cheese. Sprinkle the chopped garlic and smoked mozzarella over the toppings. Place the pizza pan on the preheated ovenstone and bake at 500 degrees F. for 20 to 30 minutes.

Remove the pizza from the oven and place on a cooling rack. Brush the edge with olive oil and sprinkle the top with Romano cheese. Remove the pizza from the pan, cut into slices and serve.

Page 94: Top Left, Traditional Deep-Dish Pan Pizza; Bottom, Pages 94 and 95, Shrimp With Pancetta Pizza; Page 95: Top, Barbecued Chicken Pizza With Black Bean Sauce; Middle, The Great Pumpkin Pizza.

PIZZA RUSTICA

Serves 6.

15 ounces ricotta cheese

8 ounces low-moisture part-skim mozzarella cheese, diced

1/2 cup chopped fresh Italian flat-leaf parsley

1 pound salami, finely diced or ground

6 ripe plum tomatoes, chopped

1/2 teaspoon dried oregano

1/2 teaspoon dried basil

1/2 teaspoon dried marjoram

2 large eggs

19 ounces Basic Pizza Dough (page 28)

Place an ovenstone on the lowest rack of the oven, closest to the heating element. Preheat at 500 degrees F. for 1 hour.

Combine all of the ingredients, except the dough, in a large bowl. Stir until well blended, then set the filling mixture aside.

Divide the dough into a 14-ounce ball and a 5-ounce ball. Set the 5-ounce ball aside. Roll the larger piece of dough into a circle 16 inches in diameter and press it into a 14-inch round deep-dish pizza pan. Pull the dough part way up the side of the pan. Spoon the ricotta mixture into the pan. Roll the 5-ounce ball into a 15-inch circle and place it on top of the filling. Press the edges together to seal the dough and make a slit in the top for ventilation.

Place the pan on the preheated ovenstone and bake at 500 degrees F. for 25 minutes. Remove the pizza from the oven and cool briefly on a wire rack. Slice with a pizza wheel and serve.

BACON CHEESEBURGER DELUXE PIZZA

Serves 4 to 6.

19 ounces Basic Pizza Dough (page 28)

8 ounces low-moisture part-skim mozzarella cheese, diced

2 to 3 tablespoons yellow cornmeal

1 pound lean hamburger, cooked and drained

Salt and freshly ground black pepper

3 ounces cheddar cheese, shredded

4 bacon strips, cooked until crisp

1 small onion, sliced into circles

16 dill pickle slices

Ketchup and yellow mustard for garnish

Place an ovenstone on the lowest rack of the oven, closest to the heating element. Preheat at 500 degrees F. for 1 hour.

Roll the pizza dough into a 14-inch circle. Sprinkle the cornmeal on a pizza peel just in the area where the pizza will lie. Place the dough on top of the cornmeal, then top with the mozzarella. Spoon the cooked hamburger over the cheese and season to taste with salt and pepper. Sprinkle the cheddar cheese on the hamburger, then arrange the bacon strips like spokes radiating from the center of the pizza. Place the onion and dill pickle slices between the bacon spokes.

Slide the pizza onto the preheated ovenstone and bake at 500 degrees F. for 10 to 14 minutes until the crust is golden. Remove the pizza from the oven and place on a cooling rack. Squirt ketchup and mustard on the top of the pizza, then slice and serve.

SPICY BEEF PIZZA WITH ROASTED GARLIC

Serves 4 to 6.

8 garlic cloves

Olive oil for brushing

1 1/2 pounds boneless sirloin or rib-eye, cut into strips

2 teaspoons chili powder

19 ounces Basic Pizza Dough (page 28)

2 to 3 tablespoons yellow cornmeal

2 teaspoons Louisiana hot sauce

8 ounces low-moisture part-skim mozzarella cheese, diced

1 medium onion, cut into rings

1 cup fresh or frozen corn kernels

1 jalapeño pepper, seeded and cut into rings

2 green onion tops, sliced

Preheat the oven to 350 degrees F.

Place the garlic cloves in an ovenproof skillet or baking dish; brush with olive oil and roast in the hot oven for 15 minutes until soft. When cool, cut the garlic cloves in half and set them aside.

Place an ovenstone on the lowest rack of the oven, closest to the heating element. Increase the temperature to 500 degrees F. and preheat for 1 hour.

Toss the beef strips in the chili powder, then arrange them in a single layer in a microwave-safe dish. Cover with plastic wrap and microwave on high for 5 minutes; do not overcook.

Roll the dough into a 14-inch square. Sprinkle the cornmeal on a pizza peel just in the area where the pizza will lie. Place the dough on top of the cornmeal, then brush it with the hot sauce. Top with the mozzarella, beef strips, onion rings, corn and roasted garlic. Arrange the jalapeño rings on the pizza, then slide it onto the preheated ovenstone. Bake for 10 to 14 minutes at 500 degrees F. until the crust is golden.

Remove the pizza from the oven and place it on a cooling rack. Garnish with sliced green onion and serve.

99

BLT PIZZA

Serves 4 to 6.

3 to 4 garlic cloves, crushed

3/4 cup mayonnaise

19 ounces Basic Pizza Dough (page 28)

2 to 3 tablespoons yellow cornmeal

8 ounces low-moisture part-skim mozzarella cheese, diced

1 pound bacon, fried until crisp

6 ripe plum tomatoes, sliced

2 ounces smoked mozzarella cheese, diced

10 ounces iceberg lettuce, julienned

"It's important to check whether your pizza is stuck to the peel before you head to the oven with it, because right or wrong once it leaves the paddle you can kiss it goodbye. There's no turning back."

Place an ovenstone on the lowest rack of the oven, closest to the heating element. Preheat at 500 degrees F. for 1 hour.

Blend the garlic and mayonnaise in a small bowl, then spoon the mixture into a squirt bottle. Reserve in the refrigerator.

Roll the pizza dough into a rectangle slightly smaller than the ovenstone. Sprinkle the cornmeal on a pizza peel just in the area where the pizza will lie. Place the dough on top of the cornmeal. Squirt some of the garlic-flavored mayonnaise onto the dough, then top it with the low-moisture mozzarella. Break strips of crisp bacon onto the pizza. Add half of the tomato slices and the smoked mozzarella. Slide the pizza onto the preheated ovenstone and bake at 500 degrees F. for 10 to 14 minutes until the crust is golden.

Remove the pizza from the oven and place it on a wire rack. Finish the pizza with a few squirts of the garlic-flavored mayonnaise, then add the lettuce and the rest of the tomato slices. Serve immediately.

CAJUN PIZZA

Serves 4 to 6.

1 pound andouille or other spicy smoked sausage

8 ounces large shrimp, peeled and deveined

1/2 cup thick tomato sauce

1 teaspoon Louisiana hot sauce, plus extra for brushing

19 ounces Basic Pizza Dough (page 28)

2 to 3 tablespoons yellow cornmeal

10 ounces low-moisture part-skim mozzarella cheese, diced

3 ripe plum tomatoes, diced

Place an ovenstone on the lowest rack of the oven, closest to the heating element. Preheat at 500 degrees F. for 1 hour.

Preheat a grill or outdoor barbecue.

Sear the andouille sausage and the shrimp on the hot grill, turning them, until scored with grill marks on both sides. Remove the sausage and shrimp from the grill and let cool. Slice the andouille and reserve with the shrimp.

In a small bowl, combine the tomato sauce and hot sauce. Thin the sauce with a little water if necessary, then set it aside.

Roll the pizza dough into a rectangle slightly smaller than the pizza stone. Sprinkle cornmeal on the ovenstone just in the area where the pizza will lie. Place the dough on top of the cornmeal and brush it with the sauce. Add the mozzarella, then top pizza with the sausage, shrimp and diced tomatoes. Slide the pizza onto the ovenstone and bake at 500 degrees F. for 10 to 14 minutes until the crust is golden.

Remove the pizza from the oven and place it on a cooling rack. Brush the edges with hot sauce, slice and serve.

MUFFULETTA PIZZA

Serves 4 to 6.

19 ounces Basic Pizza Dough (page 28)

2 to 3 tablespoons yellow cornmeal

1 cup olive salad (recipe follows)

8 ounces low-moisture part-skim mozzarella cheese, diced

4 ounces ham, thinly sliced

4 ounces hard salami, thinly sliced

Freshly grated Romano cheese for sprinkling

12 pimento-stuffed green olives, sliced

"A muffuletta is a popular New Orleans sandwich that consists of layers of thinly sliced ham, salami, Provolone and olive salad on a sesame seed bun the size of a dinner plate. There are as many different versions of this specialty as there are restaurants that serve them, but they all taste best when served warm."

Place an ovenstone on the lowest rack of the oven, closest to the heating element. Preheat at 500 degrees F. for 1 hour.

Roll the pizza dough into a 14-inch circle. Sprinkle the cornmeal on a pizza peel just in the area where the pizza will lie. Place the dough on top of the cornmeal. Spread olive salad on the dough, then top with the mozzarella. Arrange slices of ham and salami on the pizza. Slide the pizza onto the preheated ovenstone and bake at 500 degrees F. for 10 to 14 minutes until the crust is golden.

Remove the pizza from the oven and transfer it to a cooling rack. Brush the edge with oil from the olive salad and sprinkle the top with Romano cheese. Garnish with olive slices and serve.

OLIVE SALAD

2 cups pickled cauliflower

1 carrot, cut into large pieces

1 stalk celery, cut into large pieces

6 pearl onions

4 garlic cloves

1 pound pimento-stuffed green olives

8 ounces canned chick peas (garbanzo beans), drained

1/3 cup Italian flat-leaf parsley

1 teaspoon dried oregano

Salt and freshly ground black pepper

1/2 cup olive oil

Chop the cauliflower, carrot and celery in a food processor, then add the pearl onions, garlic, green olives, garbanzos, parsley and oregano. Season the mixture with salt and pepper. Pulse the machine a couple of times until the ingredients are finely chopped, then add the olive oil. Use the olive salad immediately or refrigerate it, tightly covered, for up to a week.

GREEK PIZZA ONLY BETTER

Serves 4 to 6.

19 ounces Basic Pizza Dough (page 28)

2 to 3 tablespoons yellow cornmeal

2 tablespoons Olivada spread (see note below)

8 ounces low-moisture part-skim mozzarella cheese, diced

4 to 6 large grape leaves, rinsed and patted dry

6 ounces diced Greek Kasseri cheese (white sharp cheddar can be substituted)

4 ripe plum tomatoes, thinly sliced

12 black olives, pitted and halved

4 water-packed artichoke hearts, drained and quartered

Juice of 1/2 lemon

Freshly grated Romano cheese for sprinkling

Preheat an ovenstone on the lowest rack of the oven, closest to the heating element. Preheat at 500 degrees F. for 1 hour.

Roll the pizza dough into a 14-inch circle. Sprinkle the cornmeal on a pizza peel just in the area where the pizza will lie. Place the dough on top of the cornmeal and brush it with Olivada spread. Spread the mozzarella over the dough, then lay the grape leaves on the cheese. Sprinkle Greek Kasseri cheese on top of the grape leaves. Ring the center of the pizza with tomato slices and place the black olives in the center of the ring. Dot the rest of the pizza with pieces of artichoke.

Slide the pizza onto the preheated ovenstone and bake at 500 degrees F. for 10 to 14 minutes until the crust is golden. Remove the pizza from the oven and place it on a wire rack to cool. Squeeze the lemon juice over the pizza and brush the edge with Olivada spread. Dust with Romano cheese and serve.

Note: Olivada spread is an olive paste found in specialty stores and Italian markets. If unavailable, a purée of pitted black olives and a little olive oil can be substituted.

DEEP DISH SPINACH AND EGG PIZZA

Serves 4 to 6.

19 ounces Basic Pizza Dough (page 28)

8 ounces low-moisture part-skim mozzarella cheese, diced

1/4 cup olive oil, plus extra for brushing

1 pound fresh spinach, washed and dried

15 ounces ricotta cheese

5 large eggs

4 ounces Parmesan cheese, grated

4 ounces Provolone cheese, diced

Salt and freshly ground black pepper

5 bacon strips, cooked until crisp

Place an ovenstone on the lowest rack of the oven, closest to the heating element. Preheat at 500 degrees F. for 1 hour.

Brush a 14-inch round deep-dish pizza pan with olive oil. Roll the dough into a 16-inch circle and press it into the pan, pulling the dough partially up the side to form a lip. Top the dough with half of the mozzarella and set the pan aside.

Heat 1/4 cup olive oil in a skillet and add the spinach. Cook over medium heat until the leaves wilt, then remove the pan from the heat. Stir in the ricotta, 1 egg, Parmesan and Provolone. Season the mixture with salt and pepper, then spoon it into the pan over the mozzarella.

Using the back of a spoon, make four small wells in the cheese mixture; break 1 egg into each of the wells. Crumble the bacon over the pizza and sprinkle with the remaining mozzarella. Place the pan on the preheated pizza stone and bake at 500 degrees F. for 18 to 20 minutes.

Remove the pan from the oven and place it on a wire rack. Cool the pizza for 10 to 15 minutes, then cut and serve.

THE GREAT PUMPKIN PIZZA

Serves 4 to 6.

1 large butternut squash

1 tablespoon pumpkin pie spice

1 thick slice turkey breast, about 6 ounces

Olive oil for brushing

4 ounces (1/2 cup) pine nuts

19 ounces Basic Pizza Dough

2 to 3 tablespoons yellow cornmeal

8 ounces smoked mozzarella cheese, thinly sliced

4 ounces (1/2 cup) whole cranberry sauce

"Since fresh pumpkin is only available seasonally, other varieties of winter squash including butternut and acorn can be substituted with no appreciable difference in taste."

Place an ovenstone on the lowest rack of the oven, closest to the heating element. Preheat at 500 degrees F. for 1 hour.

Cut the squash in half lengthwise and remove the seeds. Place the squash, cut side down, in a baking dish. Add 2 tablespoons water to the dish and cover with plastic wrap, turning back one corner to vent. Microwave at high until tender, about 8 minutes, rotating the dish once during cooking. Let cool, then scoop out the pulp. Place the pulp in a bowl, add the pumpkin pie spice and mash with a fork.

Baste the turkey breast lightly with olive oil, then grill, roast or microwave the meat until it is fully cooked. Set the turkey aside.

Place the pine nuts in a small skillet and toast over low heat until lightly browned. Shake the pan or stir constantly, being careful not to burn the pine nuts.

Roll the pizza dough on a floured board into a rectangle slightly smaller than the ovenstone. Spread the cornmeal on a pizza peel just in the area where the pizza will lie. Place the dough on top of the cornmeal and spread on the squash mixture. Top with slices of mozzarella. Cut the turkey into strips and arrange on the cheese. Sprinkle with toasted pine nuts.

Slide the pizza onto the preheated ovenstone and bake at 500 degrees F. for 10 to 14 minutes until the crust is golden. Transfer the baked pizza to a rack and let cool until the cheese sets, about 5 minutes. Garnish the pizza with small dollops of whole cranberry sauce, slice and serve.

REDSKIN POTATO PIZZA WITH ASPARAGUS AND GARLIC

Serves 4 to 6.

19 ounces Basic Pizza Dough

2 to 3 tablespoons yellow cornmeal

Olive oil for brushing

8 ounces low-moisture part-skim mozzarella cheese, diced

1 medium redskin potato, thinly sliced

2 garlic cloves, thinly sliced

6 asparagus spears, blanched or microwaved until tender

4 ounces Havarti, Bel Paese or Muenster cheese, thinly sliced

Freshly grated Romano cheese for garnish

Place an ovenstone on the lowest rack of the oven, closest to the heating element. Preheat at 500 degrees F. for 1 hour.

Roll the pizza dough on a floured board into a rectangle slightly smaller than the ovenstone. Spread the cornmeal on a pizza peel just in the area where the pizza will lie. Place the dough on top of the cornmeal and brush it lightly with olive oil.

Sprinkle mozzarella over the dough, then dot with the garlic. Cover the dough with potato slices and arrange the asparagus spears radiating spoke-fashion from the center of the pizza. Place slices of Havarti, Bel Paese or Muenster on top of the vegetables.

Slide the pizza onto the preheated ovenstone and bake at 500 degrees F. for 10 to 14 minutes until the crust is golden.

Remove the pizza from the oven and place it on a cooling rack. Brush the edges with olive oil and garnish with Romano cheese. Cut into slices with a pizza wheel and serve.

RAVIOLI PIZZA

Serves 4 to 6.

12 black olives, pitted

2 garlic cloves

2 tablespoons olive oil, plus extra for brushing

4 canned plum tomatoes, drained (reserve juice)

6 ounces thick tomato sauce

16 cheese-filled ravioli

19 ounces Basic Pizza Dough (page 28)

2 to 3 tablespoons yellow cornmeal

10 ounces low-moisture part-skim mozzarella cheese, diced

Freshly grated Romano cheese for sprinkling

"When it comes to pizza shapes and sizes, the recommendations on the recipes in this book are not set in stone. No matter whether you are making a round, oval, square or rectangular pizza, you must roll the dough small enough so that it won't fall over the edge of the ovenstone."

Place an ovenstone on the lowest rack of the oven, closest to the heating element. Preheat at 500 degrees F. for 1 hour.

Chop the black olives and garlic together in a food processor. Add 2 tablespoons olive oil and the plum tomatoes, then pulse the machine briefly to chop the tomatoes. Transfer the olive mixture to a bowl and add the tomato sauce. If necessary, thin the olive-tomato sauce with some of the reserved juice from the tomatoes. Set the sauce aside.

Cook the ravioli in a large pot of boiling salted water for a few minutes until the edges are tender. Remove the ravioli from the water with a slotted spoon and reserve for assembly.

Roll the dough into a rectangle slightly smaller than the pizza stone. Sprinkle a pizza peel with cornmeal just in the area where the pizza will lie. Place the dough on top of the cornmeal. Spread mozzarella over the dough, then arrange the ravioli on top of the cheese. Spoon olive-tomato sauce over the pasta. Slide the pizza onto the preheated ovenstone and bake at 500 degrees F. for 10 to 14 minutes until the crust is golden.

Remove the pizza from the oven to a cooling rack. Brush the edges with olive oil and sprinkle the top with Romano cheese. Cut with a pizza wheel, then serve.

TEX MEX PIZZA

Serves 4 to 6.

19 ounces Basic Pizza Dough (page 28)

2 to 3 tablespoons yellow cornmeal

8 ounces low-moisture part-skim mozzarella cheese, diced

4 ounces cheddar cheese, grated

1 1/2 cups fresh salsa, drained

12 black olives, pitted and halved

Olive oil for brushing

Place an ovenstone on the lowest rack of the oven, closest to the heating element. Preheat at 500 degrees F. for 1 hour.

Roll the dough into a rectangle slightly smaller than the pizza stone. Sprinkle the cornmeal on a pizza peel just in the area where the pizza will lie. Place the dough on top of the cornmeal. Spread the mozzarella on the dough, then add the cheddar cheese. Spoon the salsa onto the cheese and scatter the olives over the the pizza.

Slide the pizza onto the preheated ovenstone and bake at 500 degrees F. for 10 to 14 minutes until the crust is golden. Remove the pizza from the oven and place on a cooling rack. Brush the edges with olive oil and serve.

SOUTH OF THE BORDER PIZZA

Serves 4 to 6.

2 medium limes

6 sprigs of cilantro

2 jalapeño peppers, seeded and minced

1 medium onion, diced

1 garlic clove, diced

1 whole boneless, skinless chicken breast

19 ounces Basic Pizza Dough (page 28)

2 to 3 tablespoons yellow cornmeal

Olive oil for brushing

8 ounces low-moisture part-skim mozzarella cheese, diced

1/2 cup guacamole

1/4 cup sour cream

1 ripe plum tomato, diced

"When it comes to cilantro, there can be too much of a good thing. Unless you are a real fan of this pungent herb, use it in moderation or it will mask the flavors of your other ingredients."

Slice the limes in half and squeeze the juice into a shallow bowl. Grate the zest of one lime and add it to the bowl along with the cilantro, half of the jalapeño, the onion and garlic. Place the chicken breast in the mixture, turning it to coat the meat. Cover the dish and marinate the chicken overnight in the refrigerator.

The following day, preheat a grill or outdoor barbecue. Remove the chicken from the marinade and cook it on the hot grill until done. Remove the chicken from the grill and slice into strips. Set aside.

Place an ovenstone on the lowest rack of the oven, closest to the heating element. Preheat at 500 degrees F. for 1 hour.

Roll the pizza dough into a 14-inch circle. Sprinkle the cornmeal on a pizza peel just in the area where the pizza will lie. Brush the dough with olive oil and add the remaining jalapeño. Top with mozzarella and arrange the chicken strips on top.

Slide the pizza onto the preheated ovenstone and bake at 500 degrees F. for 10 to 14 minutes until the crust is golden. Remove the pizza from the oven and place it on a cooling rack. Mound the guacamole in the center of the pizza, then top it with the sour cream. Finish the "mountain" with a peak of diced tomato. Cut into wedges and serve.

ASIAN CHICKEN PIZZA

Serves 4 to 6.

1 whole boneless, skinless chicken breast

1/2 cup teriyaki sauce

19 ounces Basic Pizza Dough (page 28)

2 to 3 tablespoon yellow cornmeal

1 cup plum sauce

8 ounces low-moisture part-skim mozzarella cheese, diced

2 medium apples, sliced

1/2 cup bean sprouts

3 to 4 ounces water chestnuts, sliced

Place an ovenstone on the lowest rack of the oven, closest to the heating element. Preheat at 500 degrees F. for 1 hour.

Coat the chicken breast in the teriyaki sauce, then marinate it for 1 hour in the refrigerator. Cook the chicken in the microwave or oven, cut it into strips and reserve. Roll the dough into a 14-inch square. Sprinkle the cornmeal on a pizza peel just in the area where the pizza will lie. Place the dough on top of the cornmeal. Spread plum sauce on the dough, reserving 2 tablespoons of the sauce for use after the pizza has been baked. Add the mozzarella, then top the pizza with the chicken, apple, bean sprouts and water chestnuts. Slide the pizza onto the preheated ovenstone and bake at 500 degrees F. for 10 to 14 minutes until the crust is golden.

Remove the pizza from the oven and place it on a cooling rack. Brush the edges with the reserved plum sauce, then cut and serve.

CHICKEN AND OH SO MUCH GARLIC PIZZA

Serves 4 to 6.

1 whole boneless, skinless chicken breast

10 garlic cloves

1 medium onion, sliced

10 ounces Basic Pizza Dough (page 28)

Olive oil for brushing

8 ounces low-moisture part-skim mozzarella cheese, diced

2 ounces smoked mozzarella cheese, diced

2 ripe plum tomatoes, sliced

Freshly grated Romano cheese for sprinkling

Italian flat-leaf parsley for garnish

"Firming the mozzarella in the freezer before placing it in the food processor makes it easier to dice."

Butterfly the chicken breast and microwave it on high for 10 to 12 minutes. Do not overcook the chicken; the meat should be moist, not dry. When cool enough to handle, cut it into chunks. Set the chicken aside.

Preheat the oven to 350 degrees F.

Spread the garlic cloves on a baking sheet and brush them with olive oil. Bake for 15 minutes until soft, then remove the garlic from the oven and let cool. Halve the cloves and reserve for assembly.

Place an ovenstone on the lowest rack of the oven, closest to the heating element. Increase the oven temperature to 500 degrees F. and preheat for 1 hour.

Roll the pizza dough into a 14-inch square. Sprinkle the cornmeal on a pizza peel just in the area where the pizza will lie. Place the dough on top of the cornmeal and brush it with olive oil. Spread the low-moisture mozzarella over the dough. Top the pizza with chunks of chicken, roasted garlic, smoked mozzarella and tomato slices. Slide the pizza onto the preheated ovenstone and bake for 10 to 14 minutes at 500 degrees F. until the crust is golden.

Remove the pizza from the oven and place it on a cooling rack. Garnish with Italian parsley leaves and dust the top with Romano cheese. Cut with a pizza wheel, then serve.

TURKEY SAUSAGE AND APPLE PIZZA

Serves 4.

10 ounces mild turkey sausage

2 tablespoons butter

3 Golden Delicious apples, peeled, cored and cut into 1-inch cubes

19 ounces Basic Pizza Dough (page 28)

2 to 3 tablespoons cornmeal

2 tablespoons brown stone-ground mustard, plus extra for brushing

6 ounces Provolone cheese, thinly sliced

1/4 cup dried cranberries or cherries, reconstituted in hot water and drained

Place an ovenstone on the lowest rack of the oven, closest to the heating element. Preheat at 500 degrees F. for 1 hour.

Crumble the sausage into a skillet and brown it over medium heat, stirring frequently. Drain the sausage and set it aside.

In a separate skillet, melt the butter over medium heat and cook the cubed apples about 5 minutes, stirring frequently, until softened. Reserve for assembly.

Roll the pizza dough into a rectangle slightly smaller than the pizza stone. Sprinkle the cornmeal on a pizza peel just in the area where the pizza will lie. Place the dough on top of the cornmeal and brush it with 2 tablespoons mustard. Arrange slices of Provolone on the dough, then top with the sausage and apples. Slide the pizza onto the preheated ovenstone and bake at 500 degrees F. for 10 - 14 minutes until the crust is golden. Remove the pizza from the oven and place it on a cooling rack. Brush the edges with mustard, then garnish with the reconstituted cranberries or cherries. Cut into slices with a pizza wheel and serve.

SALMON AND SPINACH PIE

Serves 4 to 6.

2 pounds fresh spinach

19 ounces Basic Pizza Dough (page 28)

4 large eggs, lightly beaten

1/4 teaspoon nutmeg

10 ounces ricotta cheese

16 ounces low-moisture part-skim mozzarella cheese, diced

1 pound salmon, poached and flaked

2 tablespoons drained capers

1 teaspoon dried thyme

Olive oil for brushing

Freshly grated Parmesan cheese for sprinkling

Place an ovenstone on the lowest rack of the oven, closest to the heating element. Preheat at 500 degrees F. for 1 hour.

Wash the spinach, then steam or microwave it until wilted. Drain the spinach in a colander, then squeeze it dry and set it aside.

Roll the dough into a 16-inch circle and press it into a 14-inch round deep-dish pizza pan, pulling the dough partially up the side of the pan to form a lip.

In a mixing bowl, combine the spinach, eggs, nutmeg, ricotta, mozzarella, salmon, capers and thyme. Pour the mixture into the pizza pan. Place the pan on the preheated ovenstone and bake at 500 degrees F. for 20 to 30 minutes. Remove the pan from the oven and place it on a cooling rack. Brush the edge with olive oil, then sprinkle the top with Parmesan cheese. Let the pizza sit for 10 to 15 minutes before removing it from the pan and slicing.

TUNA PIZZA

Serves 4 to 6.

19 ounces Basic Pizza Dough (page 28)

2 to 3 tablespoons yellow cornmeal

8 ounces low-moisture part-skim mozzarella cheese, diced

6 1/2 ounces water-packed solid white tuna, drained

6 water-packed artichoke hearts, drained and halved

3 ripe plum tomatoes, sliced

1/2 small green bell pepper, seeded and cut into rings

Jalapeño pepper sauce (optional)

Freshly grated Romano cheese for sprinkling

Place an ovenstone on the lowest rack of the oven, closest to the heating element. Preheat at 500 degrees F. for 1 hour.

Roll the pizza dough into a 14-inch circle. Sprinkle the cornmeal on a pizza peel just in the area where the pizza will lie. Place the dough on top of the cornmeal. Spread the mozzarella on the dough, then top the cheese with chunks of tuna, artichokes, tomatoes and bell pepper. Slide the pizza onto the preheated ovenstone and bake at 500 degrees F. for 10 to 14 minutes until the crust is golden.

Remove the pizza from the oven and place it on a cooling rack. If desired, drizzle jalapeño pepper sauce on the pizza. Sprinkle the pizza with Romano cheese, then cut it into slices with a pizza wheel and serve.

BRUNCH PIZZAS AND DESSERTS

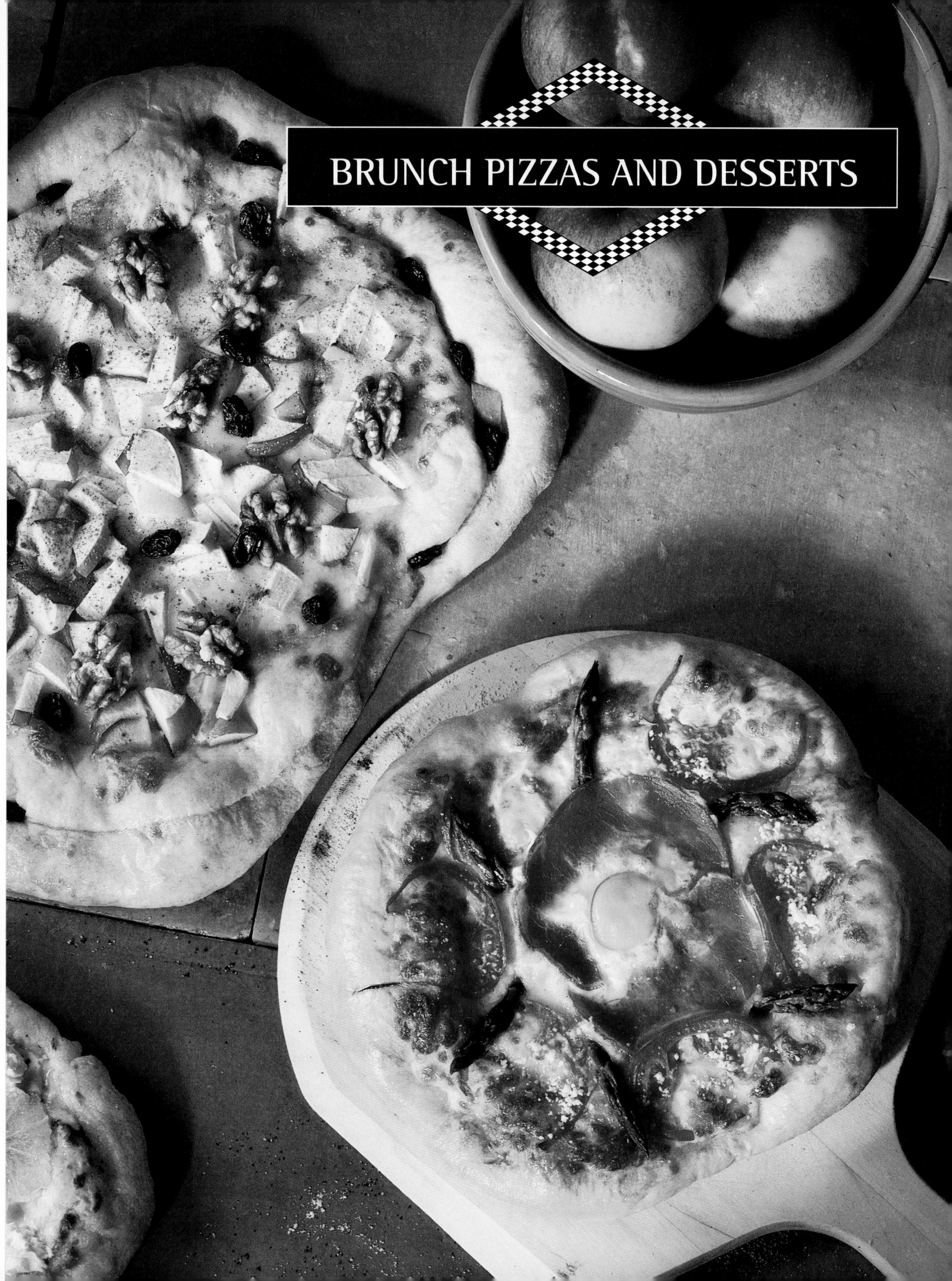

FARMER'S OMELET PIZZA

Serves 4 to 6.

19 ounces Basic Pizza Dough (page 28)

2 to 3 tablespoons yellow cornmeal

4 large eggs

4 ounces cheddar cheese, diced

6 ounces low-moisture part-skim mozzarella cheese, diced

Salt and freshly ground black pepper

1 tablespoon olive oil, plus extra for brushing

2 medium redskin potatoes, cooked until tender and diced

1 small red onion, diced

1 small green bell pepper, diced

1 small red bell pepper, diced

1 tablespoon freshly grated Romano cheese

2 ripe plum tomatoes, diced

Paprika for garnish

"Pizzas with eggs on them don't rewarm well : the eggs turn into rubber. Egg pizzas should always be eaten freshly baked."

Place an ovenstone on the lowest rack of the oven, closest to the heating element. Preheat at 500 degrees F. for 1 hour.

Roll the pizza dough into a rectangle slightly smaller than the pizza stone. Spread the cornmeal on a pizza peel just in the area where the pizza will lie. Place the dough on the cornmeal, then brush with olive oil.

In a medium bowl, beat the eggs with the cheddar and mozzarella cheese. Season the mixture with salt and pepper, then set it aside.

Heat 1 tablespoon olive oil in a skillet and sauté the potatoes, onion and bell peppers until lightly browned. Season with salt and pepper.

Spread the egg and cheese mixture on top of the pizza dough, then top with the sautéed vegetables. Slide the pizza onto the preheated ovenstone and bake at 500 degrees F. for 10 to 14 minutes until the crust is golden.

Remove the pizza from the oven and place it on a cooling rack. Brush the edges with olive oil and dust with Romano cheese. Garnish with diced tomato and paprika for color, then serve.

TEXAS BREAKFAST PIZZA

Serves 4 to 6.

2 cups cooked black beans

1 medium onion, quartered

1/4 teaspoon chili powder

12 sprigs of cilantro

1/2 cup thick tomato sauce

4 large eggs

4 ounces cheddar cheese, diced

6 ounces low-moisture part-skim mozzarella cheese, diced

3/4 cup drained salsa for garnish

Place all but 1/4 cup of the black beans in the bowl of a food processor. Add the onion, chili powder, cilantro and tomato sauce and pulse the machine to purée the mixture. Set the bean sauce aside, along with the remaining 1/4 cup black beans.

In a medium bowl, combine the eggs, cheddar and mozzarella. Set the egg mixture aside while preparing the dough.

Place an ovenstone on the lowest rack of the oven, closest to the heating element. Preheat at 500 degrees F. for 1 hour.

Roll the pizza dough into a 14-inch square. Sprinkle the cornmeal on a pizza peel just in the area where the pizza will lie. Place the dough on top of the cornmeal, then spread the black bean sauce on the dough. Top with the egg mixture. Slide the pizza onto the preheated ovenstone and bake at 500 degrees F. for 10 to 14 minutes until the crust is golden. Remove the pizza from the oven and place it on a cooling rack. Garnish with the remaining black beans and the salsa, then serve.

GRILLED RATATOUILLE PIZZA

Serves 1 to 2.

1 small onion, quartered

1 small zucchini, cubed

1 small green bell pepper, cubed

1 small eggplant, peeled and cubed

1 medium tomato, cut into wedges

1/4 cup olive oil

3 garlic cloves, diced

1/2 cup dried basil

10 ounces Basic Pizza Dough (page 28)

2 to 3 tablespoons yellow cornmeal

6 ounces low-moisture part-skim mozzarella cheese, diced

1/4 cup grated smoked mozzarella cheese for garnish

"Always bake with the logo side down on your ovenstone. Also, don't immerse the stone in water to clean it. Brush the ash from the stone and wipe it off with a damp cloth on a regular basis.

Preheat a grill or outdoor barbecue.

Alternating the ingredients, thread the zucchini, bell pepper, eggplant and tomato onto 4 skewers. Place the skewers on the hot grill and cook until the vegetables are tender, turning the vegetables frequently and watching them carefully so they don't burn. Remove the skewers from the heat and let them cool for 5 minutes.

Place an ovenstone on the lowest rack of the oven, closest to the heating element. Preheat at 500 degrees F. for 1 hour.

In a large bowl, combine the olive oil, garlic and basil. Remove the vegetables from the skewers and toss them in the basil mixture until well coated. Set the marinated vegetables aside.

Roll the dough into a 9-inch circle. Sprinkle cornmeal on the pizza peel just in the area where the pizza will lie. Place the dough on top of the cornmeal. Spread the mozzarella on the dough, then top with the marinated vegetables. Slide the pizza onto the preheated ovenstone and bake at 500 degrees F. for 5 to 8 minutes, until the crust is golden.

Remove the pizza from the oven and place it on a cooling rack. Sprinkle the smoked mozzarella on the hot pizza, slice and serve.

POTATO AND GOAT CHEESE PIZZA
WITH ROSEMARY

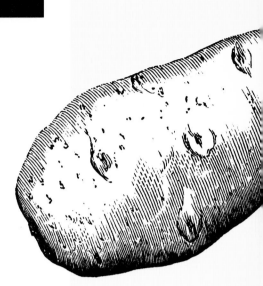

Serves 4 to 6.

2 medium redskin potatoes

3 tablespoons olive oil

Salt and freshly ground black pepper

19 ounces Basic Pizza Dough (page 28)

2 to 3 tablespoons yellow cornmeal

4 ounces low-moisture part-skim mozzarella cheese, diced

4 ounces goat cheese, cubed

2 teaspoons dried rosemary

Preheat the oven to broil.

Cut the potatoes into 1/4-inch slices. Place the potato slices on a baking sheet and brush them with olive oil. Season with salt and pepper. Broil the potato slices for 10 to 15 minutes, turning them, until partially tender and lightly browned on both sides. Remove the potatoes from the heat, then set them aside to cool.

Place an ovenstone on the lowest rack of the oven, closest to the heating element. Preheat at 500 degrees F. for 1 hour.

Roll the pizza dough into a 16-inch circle. Sprinkle the cornmeal on a pizza peel just in the area where the pizza will lie. Place the dough on top of the cornmeal. Spread the mozzarella on the dough, then arrange the potato slices on the cheese. Scatter the goat cheese over the surface and sprinkle with rosemary. Slide the pizza onto the preheated ovenstone and bake at 500 degrees F. for 10 to 14 minutes, until the crust is golden.

Remove the pizza from the oven and cool it briefly on a wire rack. Slice and serve hot.

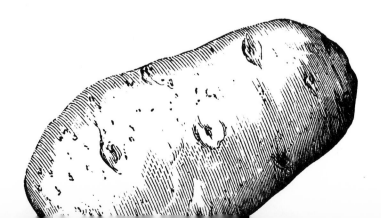

HAM AND PINEAPPLE PIZZA

Serves 4 to 6.

2 teaspoons olive oil

1 medium onion, sliced into rings

19 ounces Basic Pizza Dough (page 28)

2 to 3 tablespoons yellow cornmeal

8 ounces low-moisture part-skim mozzarella cheese, diced

8 ounces ham, thinly shaved

6 ounces canned pineapple rings, drained

2 ounces cold Fontinella cheese, grated

2 green onion tops, sliced

"My recurring nightmare is that someone puts one of my pizzas into a cardboard box and takes it away to eat later."

Place an ovenstone on the lowest rack of the oven, closest to the heating element. Preheat at 500 degrees F. for 1 hour.

Heat the olive oil in a small skillet and cook the onion rings until soft and translucent. Set the onions rings aside to cool.

Roll the dough into a rectangle slightly smaller than the pizza stone. Sprinkle the cornmeal on a pizza peel just in the area where the pizza will lie. Place the dough on top of the cornmeal. Spread the mozzarella on the dough, then top with the shaved ham. Arrange the pineapple rings on the ham, followed by the onion rings. Slide the pizza onto the preheated ovenstone and bake at 500 degrees F. for 10 to 14 minutes until the crust is golden.

Remove the pizza from the oven and transfer it to a cooling rack. Garnish with Fontinella cheese and sliced green onion tops. Cut into slices with a pizza wheel and serve.

PEARS AND GORGONZOLA PIZZA

Serves 4 to 6.

19 ounces Basic Pizza Dough (page 28)

2 to 3 tablespoons yellow cornmeal

2 tablespoons melted butter

4 ounces low-moisture part-skim mozzarella cheese, diced

2 large ripe pears, peeled, cored and thinly sliced

4 ounces of Gorgonzola cheese

1 teaspoon fresh rosemary leaves

Place an ovenstone on the lowest rack of the oven, closest to the heating element. Preheat at 500 degrees F. for 1 hour.

Roll the pizza dough into a 14-inch circle. Sprinkle the cornmeal on a pizza peel just in the area where the pizza will lie. Place the dough on top of the cornmeal. Brush the dough with some of the melted butter, then spread mozzarella over the surface. Arrange the pear slices on top of the cheese. Crumble the Gorgonzola over the pears and finish with a sprinkling of fresh rosemary. Slide the pizza onto the preheated ovenstone and bake at 500 degrees F. for 10 to 14 minutes until the crust is golden.

Remove the pizza from the oven and transfer it to a wire rack. Brush the edges with the remaining melted butter, let cool briefly, then serve.

CALIFORNIA RAISIN PIZZA

Serves 4 to 6.

19 ounces Basic Pizza Dough (page 28)

2 to 3 tablespoons yellow cornmeal

1/4 cup (1/2 stick) melted butter

6 ounces (3/4 cup) raisins

8 ounces low-moisture part-skim mozzarella cheese, diced

4 ounces Havarti or Muenster cheese, diced

1 medium Granny Smith apple

1 medium Red Delicious apple

1/2 cup chopped walnuts

1/2 teaspoon cinnamon

1 teaspoon sugar

"Stretching the dough by hand makes it tender and flaky, but rolling the dough is easier and produces better looking pizza."

Place an ovenstone on the lowest rack of the oven, closest to the heating element. Preheat at 500 degrees F. for 1 hour.

Divide the dough by weight into a 16-ounce piece and a 3-ounce piece. Set the 3-ounce piece aside.

Roll the 16-ounce piece of dough on a floured board into a rectangle slightly smaller than the ovenstone. Spread the cornmeal on a pizza peel just in the area where the pizza will lie. Place the dough on top of the cornmeal and brush it with some of the melted butter.

Place the raisins on top of the dough, then roll the 3-ounce piece of dough into a paper thin rectangle. Cover the raisins with the second piece of dough and press gently. Sprinkle with mozzarella and Havarti cheese.

Core the apples and cut them into thin slices. Arrange the apple slices on top of the cheese. Sprinkle with walnuts, cinnamon and sugar.

Slide the pizza onto the preheated ovenstone and bake at 500 degrees F. for 10 to 14 minutes until the crust is golden. Transfer the baked pizza to a wire rack and let it cool until the cheese sets, about 5 minutes. Brush the edges with butter, slice and serve.

TEMPURA-BATTERED BANANAS WITH ICE CREAM

Serves 4.

Vegetable oil for deep frying

1 package tempura batter mix

4 small ripe bananas

1 pint vanilla, praline or butter pecan ice cream

1/4 cup chopped peanuts

Heat oil in a deep saucepan or Dutch oven to 365 degrees F. In a shallow bowl, combine the tempura batter mix and water according to the package directions.

Peel the bananas and cut them in half lengthwise. Dip the slices in the batter, then fry 2 or 3 slices at a time for several minutes until golden brown. Drain on paper towels.

Serve each person 2 banana slices with a scoop of ice cream. Garnish with chopped peanuts and serve immediately.

BANANA BOAT DESSERT PIZZA

Serves 4.

10 ounces ricotta cheese

4 ounces cream cheese

1/4 cup granulated sugar

10 ounces Basic Pizza Dough (page 28)

3 bananas, sliced crosswise

2 to 3 tablespoons yellow cornmeal

Melted butter for brushing

Powdered sugar for sprinkling

4 large strawberries, sliced into fans, for garnish

"For 'thin' pizza you can use a little flour instead of cornmeal to slide the pizza off the pizza peel and onto the stone."

Preheat an ovenstone on the lowest rack of the oven, closest to the heating element. Preheat at 500 degrees F. for 1 hour.

In a medium bowl, blend the ricotta, cream cheese and sugar. Set the filling mixture aside.

Roll the pizza dough into a rectangle approximately 5 1/2 by 15-inches, then crimp the edges of the dough. Spread the cornmeal on a pizza peel just in the area where the pizza will lie. Place the dough on top of the cornmeal. Spoon the ricotta mixture down the center of the dough. Place the banana slices in the ricotta mixture and use them to push the filling toward the sides of the pizza. Leave a 1-inch plain border on each side. Brush the edge with butter. Slide the pizza onto the preheated ovenstone and bake at 500 degrees F. for 8 to 10 minutes until the crust is golden.

Remove the pizza from the oven and place it on a wire rack. Brush the edges of the pizza with melted butter and let it cool briefly, then place it in the refrigerator. When chilled, dust the pizza with powdered sugar and garnish with strawberry fans. Cut into slices, then serve.

JUST A LITTLE CHEESECAKE PIE

Serves 4 to 6.

19 ounces of Basic Pizza Dough (page 28)

2 to 3 tablespoons yellow cornmeal

15 ounces ricotta cheese

4 ounces cream cheese

1/2 cup sugar

1 large Granny Smith Apple, cored and coarsely chopped

1 banana, sliced crosswise

2 tablespoons melted butter for brushing

1 large kiwi, peeled and sliced

12 whole raspberries

1/4 cup semi-sweet chocolate chips, melted

Place an ovenstone on the lowest rack of the oven, closest to the heating element. Preheat at 500 degrees F. for 1 hour.

Roll the pizza dough into a rectangle slightly smaller than the ovenstone. Spread the cornmeal on a pizza peel just in the area where the pizza will lie. Place the dough on top of the cornmeal.

In a medium bowl, blend the ricotta, cream cheese and sugar. Spread the mixture over the dough using a spatula or the back of a large spoon. Arrange pieces of apple and slices of banana on top of the cheese mixture. Slide the pizza onto the preheated ovenstone and bake at 500 degrees F. for 10 to 14 minutes, until the crust is golden.

Remove the pizza from the oven and place on a cooling rack. Brush the edges with melted butter and arrange kiwi slices and whole raspberries on top of the pizza. Drizzle melted chocolate onto the pizza with a spoon and refrigerate. Serve the dessert pizza slightly chilled.

KEY LIME PIE PIZZA

Serves 4.

10 ounces Basic Pizza Dough (page 28)

8 ounces ricotta cheese

4 ounces cream cheese

1/2 cup sugar

Zest of 3 limes (reserve fruit for garnish)

Green food coloring (optional)

Whipped cream for garnish

"Don't be taken in by ovenstones that come with lift racks. The ovenstone is intended to be kept in the oven, not used as a serving tray."

Place an ovenstone on the lowest rack of the oven, closest to the heating element. Preheat at 500 degrees F. for 1 hour.

Roll the pizza dough on a floured board into a rectangle approximately 5 1/2 by 15-inches. Spread the cornmeal on a pizza peel just in the area where the dough will lie. Place the dough on top of the cornmeal.

In a food processor, mix the ricotta, cream cheese, sugar and lime zest. Blend until smooth, then add a drop or two of green food coloring, if desired. If the mixture is too thick to spread, adjust the consistency with the juice from one of the limes.

Spread the cream cheese mixture on the dough, then slide the pizza onto the preheated ovenstone. Bake at 500 degrees F. for 8 to 10 minutes, until the crust is golden. Cool the baked pizza for a few minutes on a rack, then place it in the refrigerator or freezer until cold.

Peel the remaining 2 limes and slice into thin rings. Dip the slices in sugar. Arrange the sugared lime slices on top of the chilled pizza, then pipe whipped cream around the edge. Cut with a pizza wheel and serve immediately.

ITALIAN PLUM DESSERT PIZZA

Serves 4 to 6.

19 ounces Basic Pizza Dough (page 28)

1/4 cup (1/2 stick) melted butter for brushing

3 pounds fresh purple plums, halved and pitted (see note below)

3/4 cup granulated sugar

1 tablespoon cinnamon

Powdered sugar for garnish

Preheat the oven to 500 degrees F.

Roll the pizza dough into a circle approximately 16 inches in diameter. Press the dough into a 14-inch round deep-dish pizza pan so that it lines the bottom and side of the pan. Brush the dough with butter. Fan the halved plums from the outside edge to the center of the pan so that the halves overlap. In a small bowl, combine the sugar and cinnamon; sprinkle the mixture over the plums. Bake for 20 minutes, then transfer the pizza to a cooling rack. Dust with powdered sugar, slice and serve at room temperature.

Note: If plums are not in season, baking apples or ripe pears can be substituted.

CINNAMON AND SUGAR FOCACCIA

Serves 4 to 6.

16 ounces Basic Pizza Dough (page 28)

1/4 cup (1/2 stick) melted butter

2 tablespoons cinnamon

3 tablespoons sugar

2 tablespoons honey

8 ounces mascarpone cheese

"Your pizza will let you know when it's done. The crust will be nicely browned both on the top and bottom, and the bottom will be slightly warped."

Place an ovenstone on the lowest rack of the oven, closest to the heating element. Preheat at 500 degrees F. for 1 hour.

Roll the pizza dough into a 14-inch circle and place it on a pizza screen. Brush the dough with butter, then notch the edge for a decorative finish. Sprinkle the dough with cinnamon and sugar. Place the screen on the preheated stone and bake the focaccia at 500 degrees F. for 8 to 10 minutes until golden brown.

While the focaccia is baking, blend the honey and the mascarpone in a small bowl. Remove the focaccia from the oven and cool briefly on a wire rack. Slice the focaccia into narrow wedges and serve with the honey and mascarpone sauce for dipping.

FRUIT FOCACCIA

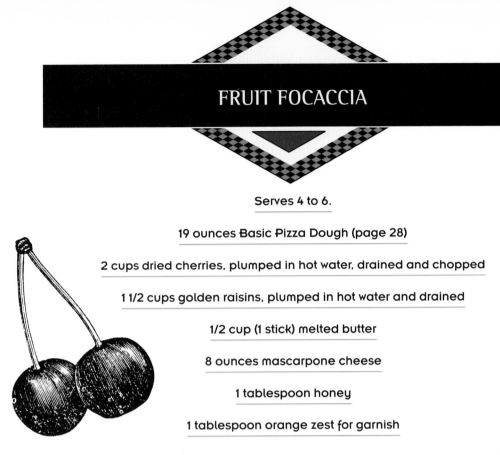

Serves 4 to 6.

19 ounces Basic Pizza Dough (page 28)

2 cups dried cherries, plumped in hot water, drained and chopped

1 1/2 cups golden raisins, plumped in hot water and drained

1/2 cup (1 stick) melted butter

8 ounces mascarpone cheese

1 tablespoon honey

1 tablespoon orange zest for garnish

Place an ovenstone on the lowest rack of the oven, closest to the heating element. Preheat at 500 degrees F. for 1 hour.

Knead the cherries and raisins into the dough and let it rise in a covered bowl for 2 hours.

Brush a 9 by 12-inch rimmed baking sheet with butter. Roll the dough into a rectangle slightly smaller than the baking sheet and press it into the pan. Brush the dough with butter, then cover the pan with plastic wrap. Let rise for 10 minutes. Place the baking sheet on the preheated ovenstone and bake the focaccia for 10 to 15 minutes until golden brown. Remove the pan from the oven and cool the focaccia on a wire rack for several minutes.

In a small bowl, combine the mascarpone and honey. Spread the mixture over the focaccia and garnish with orange zest. Cut the focaccia into slices and serve.

CANNOLI CALZONE

Makes 8 to 10 calzone.

16 ounces ricotta cheese

3/4 cup sugar, plus extra for sprinkling

1/2 cup chopped pistachios

1/2 cup miniature semi-sweet chocolate chips

1/2 teaspoon vanilla

1/4 teaspoon cinnamon, plus extra for sprinkling

2 large eggs, lightly beaten

19 ounces Basic Pizza Dough (page 28)

1/4 cup (1/2 stick) melted butter for brushing

"Calzone should be baked as soon as they are filled. Do not refrigerate or freeze them or they will become soggy. If you need to prepare calzone ahead of time, bake them about seventy-five per cent of the way, then hold them at room temperature for a few hours and finish them in the oven at the last minute."

Preheat an ovenstone on the center rack of the oven for 30 minutes at 450 degrees F.

In a medium bowl, blend the ricotta, sugar, pistachios, chocolate chips, vanilla and cinnamon. Incorporate the beaten eggs into the ricotta mixture a little at a time, adding just enough to bind the filling; the mixture should be moist but not wet. Set the filling aside.

Roll the pizza dough into a sheet about 1/4-inch thick. Cut circles of dough with a 4-inch biscuit cutter.

Place a heaping tablespoon of the filling on the center of each circle and seal the calzone following the instructions on page 29. Place the calzone on a baking sheet lined with parchment paper. Cut a slit in each calzone to vent the steam as they bake, then brush with butter and sprinkle with a little sugar and cinnamon. Bake on the preheated ovenstone for 15 to 20 minutes at 450 degrees F. until golden brown. Remove the calzone from the oven and let it cool briefly on a wire rack. If desired, garnish with whole blueberries and raspberries.

COOL CAPPUCCINO SHAKES

Serves 2.

1 pint vanilla ice cream

3 ounces cappuccino syrup

1/2 cup heavy cream

Place the ice cream and cappuccino syrup in a blender container; blend until smooth. If the drink is too thick, adjust the consistency with heavy cream. Pour the cappuccino shake into frosted glasses and garnish with whipped cream, cinnamon, chocolate chips, strawberries, peanuts or whatever you crave!

TROUBLESHOOTING

PROBLEM:

SOLUTION:

The dough won't roll out.

Never fold rested dough back into a ball. Instead, flour it, pat it flat, then roll it.

Burnt cheese/crust not done.

The stone is not hot enough. Preheat for one hour at 500 degrees F.

The dough browned too soon.

When the dough is too fresh the sugar in it caramelizes.
Let dough rest at least 3 to 4 hours before baking it.

The toppings fell through the cheese.

Use part-skim instead of whole milk mozzarella.

The dough is tough and dried out.

The oven temperature is too low and the stone is not hot enough. Preheat for one hour at 500 degrees F.

TROUBLESHOOTING

PROBLEM:

SOLUTION:

A black circle formed on the ovenstone.

Oils in commercially-made frozen pizzas stain the stone.

The stone turned black.

Too much oil on the stone. Don't put the toppings so close to the edge of the pizza. Reheat sliced pizza on foil instead of directly on the stone.

Damp, watery pizza.

Some vegetables such as green peppers and mushrooms must be precooked otherwise moisture gets trapped in the pizza.

No consistency to the crust.

The yeast was old or the dough had exceeded its life. Use dough within 24 hours of preparation.

GLOSSARY

MOZZARELLA

A highly-meltable cheese that is available in several different forms. On pizza use the low-moisture part-skim variety which is drier, harder and easier to dice.

MUENSTER

A semisoft, pale yellow, mild cheese.

OLIVADA SPREAD

An olive paste found in specialty stores and Italian markets.

OVENSTONE

A clay pizza baking stone that absorbs moisture and allows baking at higher temperatures; preheat for 1 hour on the bottom rack of a home oven.

PANCETTA

Italian bacon dry-cured with salt and pepper.

PARMESAN

A full-flavored hard cheese that is aged for at least two years, then grated or shaved. The finest Italian variety is Parmigiano-Reggiano.

PENNE

Short, tubular pasta with the ends cut diagonally. The name means "quills."

PEPPERONI

Spicy dried sausage. The most popular pizza topping in the U.S.

PESTO

A smooth purée traditionally made by pounding anchovies, nuts or fresh basil leaves with olive oil and grated Romano cheese in a mortar and pestle; the sauce can also be made in a blender or food processor.

PIZZA PEEL

A wooden baker's paddle with a long handle and a tapered edge that is used for transporting pizza to and from the oven.

GLOSSARY

PIZZA SCREEN

A heavy aluminum screen used in lieu of a pizza peel. The pizza is built on the screen, then the screen is placed on the heated ovenstone during baking.

PLUM TOMATOES

Sweet, meaty tomatoes with a moderate amount of juice and seeds.

PROSCIUTTO

Italian ham that is dry-cured for at least twenty-four months.

PROVOLONE

A molded cheese that ranges in flavor from mild to sharp depending on the length of curing.

RICOTTA

A creamy, mild curd cheese similar to cottage cheese; frequently used in fillings to bind the ingredients together.

ROMANO

An aged hard cheese with a sharp flavor that is perfect for grating.

ROTELLE

Corkscrew-shaped dried pasta.

SUN-DRIED TOMATOES

Intensely-flavored dried plum tomatoes that are sold dried or packed in olive oil. Reconstitute the dried variety in hot water before use.

YEAST, ACTIVE DRY

Granulated yeast sold in individual packages containing a scant tablespoon or in 4-ounce jars. Also available in fast-acting form.

ZEST

The thin, pith-free outer peel of citrus fruit, typically grated or julienned and added to sauces or baked goods as a flavoring.

INDEX

INDEX

INDEX